IMAGES IN STONE

BrownTrout Publishers, Inc.

San Francisco

Images in Stone
Photography by David Muench
With introduction, captions, and text by Polly Schaafsma

BrownTrout Publishers, Inc.
San Francisco

IMAGES IN STONE

Photography by David Muench

Text by Polly Schaafsma

Photographs © 1995 David Muench
Text © 1995 Polly Schaafsma

FIRST EDITION

LIBRARY OF CONGRESS CATALOGING-IN-PUBLICATION DATA

Muench, David.
    Images in stone / photography by David Muench : with introduction, captions, and text by Polly Schaafsma.
      p.   cm.
    ISBN 1-56313-604-X (Ltd. ed. : alk. paper). — ISBN 1-56313-442-X (Hardbound : alk. paper)
    1. Indians of North America—West (U.S.)—Antiquities.
2. Petroglyphs—West (U.S.)   3. Picture-writing—West (U.S.)
4. Rock paintings—West (U.S.)   5. West (U.S.)—Antiquities.
I. Schaafsma, Polly.   II. Title.
E78.W5M84   1995
978'.01—dc20   95-33116
                                             CIP

Published by BrownTrout Publishers, Inc.
P.O. Box 280070
San Francisco, California 94128-0070
PRINTED IN HONG KONG BY EVERBEST

Table of Contents

To the Ancients
Creators of Power and Beauty
whose work endures
the test of time.

PREFACE
by photographer DAVID MUENCH

PICTOGRAPHS and petroglyphs are near-universal media for ancient voices. These paintings and carvings are often supernatural and mythological traditions articulated in stone. They are testimony to 10,000 years of Native American habitation while also being beautiful expressions of the abstract and symbolic in all of us. These stone images in the landscape can provide vivid glimpses into the dawn of mankind.

For me, these primitive messages from the past are difficult to understand—no neat explanations quickly evolve—but through time, and contemplation of these sacred sites, a form of visual consciousness does arise. I feel a connectedness with these prehistoric people that indelibly marks my own consciousness—a sense of harmony, a process which leads me down a pathway of beauty. The unique rock paintings and petroglyph landscapes are a major influence in my life.

Fortunately, it can be very difficult to locate and reach many of the hidden masterpieces of rock art. Much is tucked away in sandstone canyon and arroyo, at mesa's edge, along volcanic ridges, or on rounded desert boulders, seemingly unconnected to anything—but well-connected for the "dream time" of prehistoric creators of magic abstractions on rock.

Some sites that I have never located—and may never visit—are hidden forever from my visual experience; but I sense and feel their visual power anyway. Experience of this ancient landscape is an ongoing affair in time, even as they are timeless images. They stare at me through the ages—a glimpse back through history and pre-history. Their isolation is in time and space—a fragment from the past. After all, the very air we breathe, the world we view, was once breathed by these ancients, once viewed by all former living things.

As beautiful and compelling as the rock art panels are, another force is also required to illuminate their meanings. My impressions of the complex rock art landscape need more depth and sensitivity to match the power felt in many of these sacred places. Light—the luminous qualities of light, and the visual strength of light, are what helped delineate the ancient art forms for contemporary photographic expression. These qualities of light were my spirit helpers!

Directions for locating petroglyph and rock painting sites have been purposely left out to help protect them and out of respect for Native Americans' religious and ancestral traditions.

This portfolio of color images will help us see and remember a beauty and harmony that went before—help us remember, and after we are gone—preserve for those who survive, a distinctive voice of native spirituality. We hope, too, that the photographs will convey a rich, primal power that we have come to associate with the timeless subject that is the rock art landscape.

ACKNOWLEDGEMENTS

I have enjoyed great assistance in locating many of the hidden away rock art galleries along what continues to be an extraordinary journey. Without sincere encouragement and guidance, discovering and photographing this collection of images would not have been possible. Special thanks to the following people for their generous help.

Curtis Schaafsma, Museum of Indian Arts and Culture, Laboratory of Anthropology, Santa Fe – New Mexico sites

Manfred and Betsy Knaak – Anza Borrego Desert State Park sites

Fran Rugg, Anna & Kenneth Pringle, and Jim Baird, Naval Ordinance Test Station – Coso Range petroglyph sites

Robert C. Reyes and Joseph Labadie, Amistad NRA – Lower Pecos River Region

Bill Cannon, BLM, Lakeview – Warner Valley sites

Janine McFarland and Stephen Horne, USFS, Santa Barbara – Los Padres National Forest Chumash sites

Michael and John Poe – San Emigdiano Chumash paintings

Harry Crosby – Baja Mural Region

Polly Schaafsma – Baja Mural Region

Charlie DeLorme, Wild Rivers Expeditions – Baja Mural Region

Brant Calkin and Susan Tixier, Southern Utah Wilderness Alliance – Southern Utah sites

Kim Watson and Bruce Anderson – Wupatki National Monument sites

The Rangers at Petrified Forest National Park

Dr. Ed Krupp, Griffith Observatory – Burro Flats / Rocketdyne site

Dave Kaiser, BLM, Bakersfield – Carrizo Plain Chumash painting sites

Tom Alex – Big Bend National Park sites

Janet Ross, Four Corners School – San Juan River sites

Anasazi hand-holding stick figures, Grand Gulch, Utah

ART IN THE LANDSCAPE

AN INTRODUCTORY ESSAY BY POLLY SCHAAFSMA

ROCK ART - paintings and petroglyphs on stone found in the landscape where originally created - is often associated with the supernatural realm, and is sometimes thought to be the work of the gods themselves. There are Navajo mythological accounts about the Hero Twins leaving their images on the cliffs at the junction of the Pine and San Juan Rivers in northern New Mexico, The-Place-of-the-Meeting-Waters. In a rock shelter north of Canyon de Chelly in Arizona, human forms painted in pastel clays and mineral pigments that archaeologists associate with the Anasazi Basketmakers, have been described by Navajos as the work of the Navajo Gods. Likewise, the Salish in the forested river valleys of British Columbia say that the largest and oldest rock paintings of their area were made by Xwekt'xwektl, an important supernatural and teacher from the Mythological Age. Among the Kawaiisu of the western Great Basin in California, the Rock Baby, a supernatural associated with a cave that leads to the Underworld, also paints images on rocks. The Rock Baby not only paints these figures but is continually at work on them, so that they change with each human visit. Narratives that place the origin of rock art in myth time or "in the time of the beginning" and attribute these

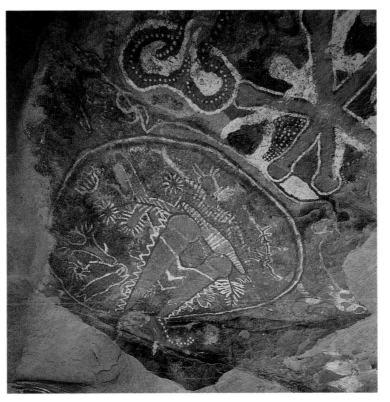

The most spectacular rock paintings in California were made by the Chumash in the southern Coastal Range and adjacent inland ranges. These complex polychrome designs are believed to relate to vision quest rituals by shamans, religious practitioners who seek spiritual power via ecstatic trance and personal encounters with supernatural forces. These sites are only a few hundred years old, and some, such as this one, are believed have been painted in historic times.

images to the work of supernatural beings contribute to the mystery that surrounds these enigmatic figures.

Paintings in rock shelters and overhangs were made from mineral pigments mixed with water or other fluids using fingers, husks, and brushes made from available natural fibers to distribute the color. Petroglyphs on cliffs, boulders, and even bedrock were made by carving designs into rock surfaces by pecking, scratching, or rubbing with stone tools. Together, these two kinds of imagery are broadly known as "rock art." Rock art was made for many different purposes and by every culture, from simple hunter-gatherer groups to sedentary horticultural societies with complicated social organizations.

Rock paintings and petroglyphs are near-universal media of human expression. Dispersed throughout the landscape, they constitute by far the most prevalent art remains from prehistory. Although petroglyphs and rock paintings are found in many parts of North America, they are more numerous in the arid West, because the dry conditions foster their preservation. In addition, the exposed rock faces, which were these artists' canvases, were readily available. Surfaces blackened by rock varnish, a dark patina that forms on rock faces in desert regions, proved to be especially conducive to the production and development of rock art images.

Rock art was not produced as a pure artistic expression for its own sake, but was part of ritualistic and social activities necessary to life. Many paintings and petroglyphs were made in the context of specific rituals and ceremonies, and in some cases were made to honor or communicate with the supernaturals themselves. The subjects of this imagery are often the symbols of prehistoric cosmologies and systems of belief. As such, rock art is a valuable part of the archaeological record that provides a wealth of information about world views and religion and related practices of ancient societies.

Rock art also offers other kinds of information. It is a sensitive archaeological tool. Examined in its many stylistic manifestations, rock art can be useful for identifying historical and cultural relationships over time and space, patterns of prehistoric communication, evidence of idea exchange, and other types of cultural contact. There are literally hundreds of rock art styles to be found in the deserts, plateau uplands, and rocky river canyons of the West. Every cultural group has developed its own mode or fashion of image-making, each with its own aesthetic dynamic. Normally that which is represented and how it is pictured will conform to culturally agreed upon values and specific methods and "rules" of representation. Even abstract patterns and the way that they are used adhere to cultural expectations.

In spite of these stylistic canons, the fact that no two figures are ever exactly alike contributes to their dynamic quality and visual interest. The painters and carvers applied their brushes and stone chisels to the rock surfaces with an enviable sense of the visual effects of their creations. These figures cut and painted on stone continue to captivate us with their universal appeal communicated through color, texture, line, and form.

In North America the oldest rock art goes back several thousand years. Recent efforts to date rock carvings by absolute methods suggest that certain petroglyphs are the work of Paleo-Indians at the end of the Pleistocene. There are, however, no North American examples of Pleistocene animals such as mammoths, musk ox, tapirs, long-horned bison, camelids, or horses. Much more work on dating rock art by absolute means is needed before the earliest petroglyphs can be assigned to Late Pleistocene big game hunters and gatherers with any degree of certainty.

There is no question, however, that later foragers were producing rock art for several thousand years before the beginning of the first millennium. In the desert regions of Baja California, the Great Basin, and northern Colorado Plateau of Western North America this life-style, referred to in archaeological literature as the Western Archaic, continued right up until the time of historic contact. These small hunter-gatherer bands can be traced in the archaeological record through the ashy remains of their campfires, fire-cracked rocks used in cooking,

and the stone tools and debris, or lithics, scattered in open sites. Sometimes there are also grinding stones (manos and slab metates) for processing wild seeds. In dry caves remnants of cordage, nets, baskets, sandals, and other perishable items have been preserved, although the material culture of foraging groups was never extensive. For these people of meager material possessions, rock painting and petroglyph making were an extremely important means through which they were able to express their complex cosmologies and world views,

Concentric circles and Rio Grande style kachina masks near Abo Pueblo ruin, New Mexico.

giving visual form to metaphors of belief. A significant number of the rock art styles produced by hunter-gatherers are among the most powerful and sophisticated art styles preserved from the past, not only in North America but in Australia and Africa as well. This hunter-gatherer rock art often represents major investments of labor, group effort, and social coordination.

Among the outstanding American rock art traditions produced by Western Archaic societies are the Great Mural paintings of central Baja California and the Coso Representational style in the desert ranges of southern California. The ages of these styles are uncertain, although both may date from the Late Prehistoric period, or after A. D. 500. The considerably older Barrier Canyon style and related paintings from Grand Canyon (estimated dates: 4000 to 500 B.C.) are notable examples of hunter-gatherer rock art on the Colorado Plateau. In the Pecos River region and the lower Rio Grande in West Texas, the Pecos River style paintings harken back to hunter-gatherer origins nearly 4000 years ago.

All of these art styles feature shamanic figures as central themes. Shamans were religious leaders that used techniques of ecstasy and trance for supernatural travel, thereby obtaining power with which to perform feats of curing, weather control, or hunting success for the benefit of the group. Such persons were healers, keepers of traditions, and maintainers of social equilibrium, as well as artists. It was the task of the shaman-artist

Mask details indicate that these Pueblo figures could date from the early 1300s.

or shaman-initiate to communicate through art to other members of his or her society or to supernaturals on the spiritual plane. In this way he/she served to visualize the journey in concrete form and validate his or her experiences. This need may explain much of the rock art that embodies shamanic subject matter. Such rock art depicts the stuff of culturally conditioned dreams and visions, experiences induced through the use of plant derived hallucinogenic agents, chanting, drumming, fasting and dehydration, lack of sleep, and other types of physical stress.

The Great Mural artists of the central Baja California sierra were desert and coastal foragers. Their rock art consists of life-sized paintings made with locally abundant pigments derived from iron and manganese oxides and gypsum. Gathering and processing the raw materials necessary for these paintings took considerable time and effort. These paintings fill rock overhangs with dynamic red and black friezes of deer, bighorn sheep, birds, marine fauna, and human beings. The human figures and animals in the Baja murals are amazingly life-like in their naturalistic silhouette forms. The static human figures in black and/or red stand with arms upraised. Ethnographic accounts tell us that this was a trance position. In contrast to the static human forms is the sense of action and movement in the animals. A shamanic model of interpretation suggests that these animals represent spirit helpers, tutelary deities, or escorts on the shamanic journey.

Equally as dramatic in the Alta California desert are the large and numerous petroglyphs of sheep and shaman figures that cover the talus boulders in certain Coso Range canyons. According to various sources these mountains were a power center for weather control shamans, whose spirit helpers, in turn, were bighorn sheep. The Cosos were regarded as a particularly auspicious locality from which to pray for rain, and there petroglyphs were made in abundance. These associations account for the large numbers of sheep, shamans, and ritual objects found

in the petroglyphs where the inextricable link between religion and landscape is realized through rock art.

The Barrier Canyon style and polychrome Pecos River paintings feature anthropomorphic forms whose stylized heads, elongation, and disproportionate limbs or even total lack of arms and legs removes them from the realm of the ordinary. Distortion and the exaggeration of certain features are artistic devices that create psychological distance between the observer and the observed. Trance, metaphorical death, magic flight, and transformation are the subject matter of these paintings. In many cases, the artist has shown a close relationship between the shaman figures and animals and birds by surrounding the protagonist, possibly himself, with his animal spirit helpers. Small figures of birds, mountain sheep, insects, and other unidentifiable life forms flank or fly toward and away from the shamanic forms. These auxiliary figures are believed to represent entities that assist the shaman in his search for supernatural power. Others may be tutelary or guardian deities, escorts, or even the shaman himself transformed.

Other rock art notable for its shamanic subject matter is the Dinwoody tradition, or Interior Line style petroglyphs, found in the Wind River Range in Wyoming. The oldest figures in this tradition are believed to be two to three thousand years old, but others are more recent. The bird and human figures that constitute the major elements are pecked in outline, while interior space is filled with parallel and wavy lines, small circles, and dots. Arms and legs of the anthropomorphic forms tend to be very short, and hands are often shown to be attached to the shoulders with fingers splayed. Stylistic similarities between these petroglyphs and Archaic rock art styles found to the south are sometimes apparent.

The Colorado River drainage includes two major tributaries, the Green and the San Juan Rivers. In this large area, shamanic themes and traditions are perpetuated in the rock art of some of the horticulturalists who lived in small villages and grew maize and squash. These groups include the earliest Anasazi farmers, the San Juan Basketmakers (400 B. C. to A. D. 600), and later more northern Fremont farmers (A. D. 600 to 1300). In general, Basketmaker and Fremont styles feature large broad-shouldered human figures, sometimes elaborately costumed with striking headgear. San Juan Basketmaker figures wear towering headdresses, necklaces, and they often hold objects such as medicine bags or human heads in their drooping hands. Some late Basketmaker (A. D. 300 - 600) figures are shown with birds either on or in place of their heads, signifying their power of shamanic flight to celestial realms. Other transformational themes include humans with animal or bird hands and feet.

Fremont anthropomorphs commonly wear antlered headgear, signifying supernatural power, as well as the necklaces common to Basketmaker art. Their held-in-hand paraphernalia also includes human heads.

Related to the shamanic or vision quest experience is a profusion of abstract elements in rock art thought to depict *entoptic* phenomena, neuro-psychological patterns seen during altered states of consciousness. These patterns include grids, dots, rayed figures, zigzags, sets of lines, circles, diamonds, and so forth. Much of the rock art just described includes such elements along with figurative subjects, although sites such as Painted Grotto in Carlsbad Caverns National Park and the Polychrome Abstracts in the San Rafael Reef feature this type of element almost exclusively.

Notable for this type of "subjective" subject matter are the colorful polychrome paintings of the Chumash of southern California. The Chumash lived in areas of easy foraging as well as in proximity to the rich resources of the sea. A secure economic base contributed to the development of Chumash village life and a distinctive society significantly more complex than social organizations sustained by hunter-gatherer bands of the arid interior. Members of the 'antap cult, or shaman-priests, were the religious leaders in Chumash society in historic times, and probably in prehistory as well. It is believed that they were responsible for the paintings and that this rock art involved interaction with the supernatural world. Chumash rock paintings found in secluded caves in south coastal California and nearby inland regions contain figures related to vision quests, and are said to depict spirits that first came to the shaman-artists in dreams. Ethnographic accounts tell us that rock art for the Chumash indicated the presence of often dangerous supernatural powers and that it also served to connect the community with its mythic past.

These paintings are not thought to be more than several hundred years old, and some were made during the last century or two. As elsewhere, iron oxides were the source of red and yellow paints, while white paint was made from diatomaceous earth. Manganese oxide provides black. Lumps of this pigment as well as cakes of hematite have been found in the Chumash region.

Elements of Chumash rock art include numerous large, highly decorative circles with intricate zigzag patterns inside, simple concentric circles, circle and diamond chains, lines of nested chevrons, dots and triangles, and criss-crossed elements. Figurative subjects are often embellished with dots. All of these elements fulfill the category commonly referred to as "entoptic." The ritual use of *Datura*, a genus of poisonous plant, is thought to have inspired some of the elements of this rock art. Representational elements in Chumash rock art include a variety of insect-like, aquatic, and reptilian life-forms that are believed to represent metaphorical concepts.

In the Southwest long before the turn of the first millennium A. D., people began planting corn (maize) and squash, cultigens that were eventually supplemented with beans and in warmer regions with cotton. Farming assured a more reliable food supply. By the turn of the

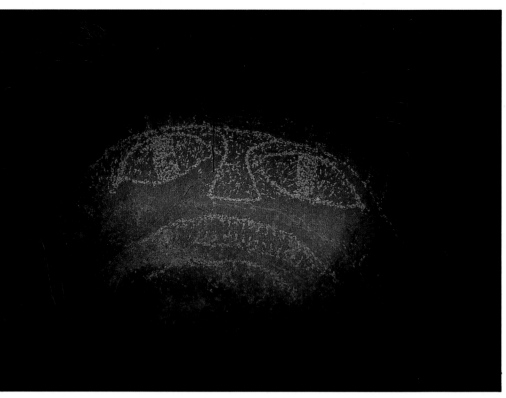

Jornada Mogollon style mask, Chihuahuan Desert

first millennium, or a little earlier in some areas, horticulture contributed to a settled life-style with associated amenities such as the development of substantial and more permanent housing. Pottery making soon followed.

Archaeologically these farmers are divisible into three major cultural groups identified with different regions. The Hohokam lived in the Lower Sonoran desert of southern Arizona, farming the riverine flood plains, aided by means of complex irrigation works. The Mogollon farmed the forested uplands and deserts to the east. The Anasazi ancestors of today's Pueblo Indians, made their homes on the cooler high mesas and canyons to the north in the Rio Grande Valley and the Colorado Plateau. Smaller, culturally distinct groups included the Sinagua of north central Arizona, the Cohonina south of the Grand Canyon, and the Hakataya in the Great Basin and Lower Colorado River desert of western Arizona. The Sinagua culture came into being about A. D. 675, reaching its height between 1150 and 1250. The Sinagua combined cultural features of both the Anasazi and the Hohokam. All of these prehistoric cultures are distinguished in the archaeological record by their material culture, most notably their shelters and pottery. In addition, each group had its own modes of graphic expression including distinctive styles of rock art. Differences in the content of this rock art and changes through time reveal distinctive, yet sometimes related, ideologies as well as growth and change in cosmologies and world views over the centuries.

The earliest Anasazi rock art on the Colorado Plateau, that of the San Juan Basketmakers, was discussed above in the context of shamanism Shamanic themes, seemingly derived from earlier hunter-gatherer groups, set the stage for an early San Juan Anasazi cosmology and the rock paintings and petroglyphs that expressed those views. After A. D. 500 or so, shamanic themes gradually disappeared to be eventually replaced with or even incorporated into action scenes that depict small dancing groups, lines of hand-holding figures, processions, people in lines carrying packs, and other small anthropomorphs interacting in a variety of ways. The fluteplayer represented on the Colorado Plateau and in the Rio Grande valley of New Mexico for almost 2000 years by the Anasazi and their Pueblo descendants is a mythological personality. Often depicted with a humpback and referred to as "Kokopelli," he is above all a symbol for fertility and the related concerns of warmth, moisture, rain, seeds, and general abundance and consequent well-being. He sometimes has insect-like qualities and is often phallic. Likewise, mountain sheep, hunting scenes, and various birds are found from Basketmaker times to A. D. 1300. Anasazi rock art between A. D. 1000 and 1300 on the Colorado Plateau is distinguished by the presence of sheep, spirals, lizards, stick figures, and textile and pottery motifs. Sinagua rock art between A.D.1150 and 1300 is very much like that of the neighboring Anasazi with more emphasis on large textile patterns.

In the lower desert region to the south, Hohokam rock art throughout this period is filled with spirals, lizards, and a few human stick figures and sheep, in addition to a variety of curvilinear abstract designs. Some of these are highly formalized pottery motifs, but the majority are vague and defy analysis, resembling more closely the preceding informal curvilinear abstracts that characterize earlier hunter-gatherer rock art in that area.

Around A. D. 1050 the Jornada style appeared in the Mogollon

Animated stick figures, Anza Borrego Desert State Park

area of the Chihuahuan Desert of southern New Mexico. The advent of this style can be dated through its expression in the figurative elements on Mimbres pottery. The elements of Jornada rock art differed significantly not only in the way they were represented but in subject matter from earlier styles in the south and in the Anasazi world to the north. This style signaled the beginning of a new artistic tradition and social institutions that have persisted into contemporary times among the Pueblos of Arizona and New Mexico. A contemporary link to the modern Pueblos provides an avenue for understanding the significance of these images. Life forms are drawn in outline, formalized interior designs are common, and heads are given full treatment with eyes, mouth, and often teeth clearly indicated. Animals in this style were represented for their metaphorical significance. The horned serpent, a deity that combines terrestrial and celestial symbolism, is represented in this rock art. A salient feature of the Jornada style is the mask which is a prelude to the development of the kachina cult among the Pueblos in the early 1300s.

Kachinas are compelling subjects in Pueblo rock art beginning around A. D. 1300. Kachinas may assume many different forms but in general are supernaturals with ancestral overtones that mediate between the Pueblo people and their gods for rain. Their masks are sometimes decorated with cloud and rain symbols, although their specific meanings are often complex and esoteric. Masked dancers in modern Pueblos embody the spirits of the kachinas they impersonate. Kachina "homes" are thought to be in lakes or near mountain tops from whence rain comes. Along with the kachinas in the Rio Grande style, deities and other supernaturals such as the horned and feathered serpent are also pictured. In addition, animals such as mountain lions, bears, water birds, and eagles are represented for their complex symbolic values. In the Pueblo world the mountain lion, bear, wolf, eagle, badger, and mole have directional significance and special curing capabilities, or are regarded as gods presiding over their specified regions. Among contemporary Pueblos the horned serpent is said to be in charge of all underground water, and he has the power to evoke floods and earthquakes if displeased with human behavior. In rock art he is associated with four-pointed stars and has celestial affiliations as well.

Shields and shield-bearing warriors are important in the Rio Grande style. They are decorated with celestial references such as sun, stars, and eagles. Shield figures are found throughout the rock art of the Pueblo region between A.D. 1325 and 1680, but shields and shield-bearing warriors are particularly well developed as a theme in the area occupied by the Southern Tewas, a linguistic division that before the Pueblo revolt was centered in the Galisteo Basin, south of Santa Fe.

Navajo rock art in northwestern New Mexico south of the San Juan River, dating from the early eighteenth century, was inspired by Pueblo art styles and a cosmological scheme that borrowed heavily from

Pueblo sources. The subject of this rock art is religious in content; Navajo supernaturals known as *ye'i* are portrayed in much of this rock art. Maize plants and clouds figure prominently because they, too, are significant in Navajo ceremonies.

Other late Proto-historic/early historic rock art in the Southwest includes that of the Apaches in southern New Mexico and West Texas and the Utes in southeastern Utah. Horses and riders and even historic events may be portrayed in this rock art, although more esoteric cultural symbolism is often included.

Basically, rock art is an artifact of ideas. It is a visual record from ancient societies that consists largely of images from the realm of the sacred, symbols of former cognitive universes. These images on stone gave substance to visions, beliefs, cosmologies, gods, and other supernaturals. Petroglyphs and rock paintings served as means to communicate myths, stories, cultural values, and abstract ideas from one generation to the next. Yet even members of the authoring group may have been subject to the ambiguity latent in rock art symbols—symbols that are rendered even more powerful by their multivocality. As symbols, rock art elements, such as the Pueblo animals in the Rio Grande style, embrace several inter-related meanings, even to those well-versed in any given iconographic system. Today the potential for understanding any given rock art style varies and may depend on whether or not the system of beliefs behind the art have been preserved by descendants of the carvers and painters whose work we are viewing. As we have seen, late Pueblo rock art in the upper Rio Grande valley, for example, is subject to more extensive interpretation than are the petroglyphs from the Gila River in Arizona. We have also seen that many near-universal patterns in shamanistic thinking can be applied to hunter-gatherer rock art to help make it more understandable.

To varying degrees, rock art imagery allows us a peek at the complicated ideology and underlying social fabric that wove cultures into patterned wholes. Since most of it relates to elaborate world views and mythologies no longer accessible, we must accept that the meaning of most rock art is either unknowable, or understandable in only the most general terms. One thing we can be sure of is that it stems from a non-material world every bit as complicated as our own.

Over time one sees that rock surfaces with carved and painted images are altered daily and seasonally by dynamic shifts in sunlight and

Shamanic figures, Nine Mile Canyon, Utah

shadow or rain and snow, all of which provide a uniquely dramatic, constantly changing theater for this landscape art form. In contrast to most forms of prehistoric art that have survived the passage of time, rock paintings and petroglyphs remain firmly fixed where they were created, within a landscape to which they are or were conceptually linked. To newcomers to this ancient continent this "wild" imagery may seem to be randomly scattered through deep canyons, across walls of sandstone, and through boulder fields black with desert varnish. As one explores cliff faces above rocky talus slopes, scrambles through brush and across the stony debris of geologic disintegration, or climbs high ledges and escarpments in search of rock art, one becomes transformed from a passive observer to an active participant *experiencing* these sites, even if the figures themselves remain ambiguous in their meaning. One may discover through this exercise that figures tend to cluster on boulders and cliffs in specific localities. Rock art is often connected with river junctions, buttes, caves, springs, and unusual volcanic formations. In some cases rock paintings and petroglyphs are framed within a form dictated by the shape of a single boulder or rock face.

If petroglyphs and rock paintings originally functioned to invest the landscape with power, they also clothed it with meaning for those that were to follow. Today, rock paintings and petroglyphs in forgotten, abandoned, and unexpected places redefine a landscape that in the last century or two has been rewritten by highways, cities, and the technological ideology of our time. Viewed in their landscape settings, images in stone emphasize for the contemporary pilgrim a sense of special place, just as rock art as originally conceived was related to native concepts regarding a particular location.

From ethnographic accounts and inference we can postulate that rock art in the southwest, the Great Basin, and elsewhere, was not distributed randomly in the landscape by its makers. Instead its occurrence correlates with places of power or cultural significance. Vision quest sites and shrines are good examples, where certain powers were to be concentrated and encountered. The Navajo Place-of-the-Meeting-Waters mentioned earlier was not only the location where the Hero Twins left their images but also where they resided after making the world safe for human life. Native ideas concerning the landscape are further complicated by the concept of a multi-layered cosmos—the view that the earth's surface is one in a series of vertical worlds, situated between the Sky and Underworlds, throughout which there is complex interaction and communication. All of these realms are inhabited by spiritual beings that affect life on the flat earth-surface plane. In some cases, as in the Pueblo region, rock art was made to reinforce these associations.

In the Pueblo world paintings and petroglyphs were made near landscape features with particular mythic significance or at shrines where communication with the supernatural world was ritually carried out. Many shrines were near villages. Others were located on high topographic features; in contrast, certain caves and rock shelters were regarded as entryways or openings to the Underworld, that was, in turn, inhabited by powerful supernaturals. In the Navajo world, rock art also commemorated locations of important mythic events, thereby reinforcing their ties to the landscape, myth-history, and cultural beginnings. As in the case of shamanic rock art, power and its mediation was and still is an important characteristic of these sites.

Thus, some sites continue to be laden with ritual significance and to communicate traditional knowledge to the descendants of the people who painted and carved the figures on the rocks. This enigmatic imagery with its compelling lines, patterns, and sometimes awesome figures continues to evoke responses not only from Native Americans but also from those of us who have lost our historical connection to our ancestor's histories on other continents. In our fascination with rock art in the landscape are we seeking a link with the places in which we now live, a landscape increasingly threatened with subjugation and development? Do we instinctively seek out these relationships to keep our balance in a rapidly changing world? Are we searching for something on the verge of being lost, just as the landscape painters of 19th century Europe were determined to record a landscape they thought was soon to disappear in the advent of the industrial revolution?

Rock art imagery continues to silently communicate and we as viewers respond. By photographing it or copying it into sketchbooks, we continue a dialogue with the past. In the course of this interaction, the rock art becomes to some degree a part of ourselves. As art historian and critic Lucy Lippard has said, "Certain forms have survived the millennia as the vehicles for vital expression. The concentric circle, the spiral, the meander, the zigzag, the lozenge or diamond shape …are still meaningful to us, even if we cannot cite their sources and symbolic intricacies."

Rock art has been preserved in the places where it was made for hundreds and in some cases thousands of years. Recordings of it have the potential for communicating this imagery to a wider audience than would otherwise be possible, and for bringing together masses of data for scientific study. Nevertheless, in comparison to the images on the rocks, copies on film and paper have to be regarded as temporary records, in spite of the fact that weathering and erosion relentlessly continue at the sites themselves. Ironically, the greatest threat to rock art in its landscape setting is man. Every effort needs to be made to protect this diverse record of past ideologies and cultures from vandalism by individuals, and complete destruction in the name of economic and industrial growth.

—Polly Schaafsma
March, 1995
Santa Fe, New Mexico

Birthing scene, Kane Springs Canyon, Utah

GREAT BASIN & MOHAVE DESERT

THE Great Basin is a rather loosely defined area of the American West. This discussion is concerned with the region that falls within the Basin and Range Province between the Sierra Nevada and the Wasatch Range, from the Mohave Desert in the south to the Black Rock Desert of southern Oregon. North-south trending ranges of fault block mountains are characteristic of this landscape. At the mouths of mountain drainages, gravelly alluvial fans are formed that coalesce into aprons at the foot of the sierras, and below are the alkali beds and dry lakes that characterize the basin floors. Coniferous forests are found in the mountains, followed by scrub oak, pinyon, juniper, sagebrush, and grasslands as one descends to lower elevations.

Great Basin prehistory goes back at least 10,000 years. The life style found in the Great Basin is generally defined as Western Archaic, a common ancient hunter-gatherer tradition within which regional divisions developed through time. This simple way of life persisted into the historic era.

The climate is characteristically arid, but because of the huge variations in elevation, the plant and animal life found in the Great Basin is diverse. Nevertheless, the environment in the Great Basin was demanding, and life was precarious. People lived in small family groups and foraged within a traditionally defined territory, moving according to what food resources were seasonally available. Seeds, pinyon nuts, and roots were major food resources throughout much of the Great Basin, and in the south, mesquite pods, ground and made into cakes, formed a staple. In the southern mountains, bighorn sheep were not only the most important large game animal, but also took on symbolic significance as is suggested by the petroglyphs in the region.

Much of the rock art in the southwestern Great Basin, such as the Coso Range petroglyphs, reflects the shamanistic practices that prevailed. The gaining of supernatural power through vision quests and dreams and the acquisition of spirit helpers were important enterprises in an attempt to exert some kind of control over an unpredictable universe. Rock art was made as part of the process of interacting with the supernatural and as a document of the shamanic journey.

On the eastern edge of the Great Basin between the end of the 9th century and ca. A. D. 1250, village dwelling Fremont Indians, added the legacy of their distinctive ideology, manifested archaeologically as horned shamanic figures, to the rock art of that region.

Fertility symbolism and other petroglyphs cover a section of volcanic tuff in central Nevada. The horizontal scoring was cut across earlier designs. The date of these figures is unknown.

A pit-and-groove boulder at Grimes Point, Nevada. Great Basin Curvilinear style petroglyphs are visible on the right. Pits and grooves are an ancient method of manipulating rock surfaces. This method was used in the Great Basin dating back several thousand years. Contrasting patinas indicate that the curvilinear designs, more recent than the pits, vary in age.

Human figures, with complex interior body patterns, representing shamans. They carry weapons in their hands, and the largest figure wears an elaborate head-dress possibly made of quail topknots.

Four bighorn sheep and a winged (?) figure superimposed on much older petroglyphs on a boulder in the Coso Range, Nevada. Boat-shaped sheep with curved legs and horns in frontal view characterize this Late Prehistoric (post A. D. 500) Coso Range style. These petroglyphs and others in this style, including elaborate anthropomorphs representing shamans, were made by hunter-gatherers that made their living on seeds, nuts, berries, edible greens, and small game.

Bighorn sheep petroglyphs covered
with orange lichen on basalt boulders,
Coso Range, California.

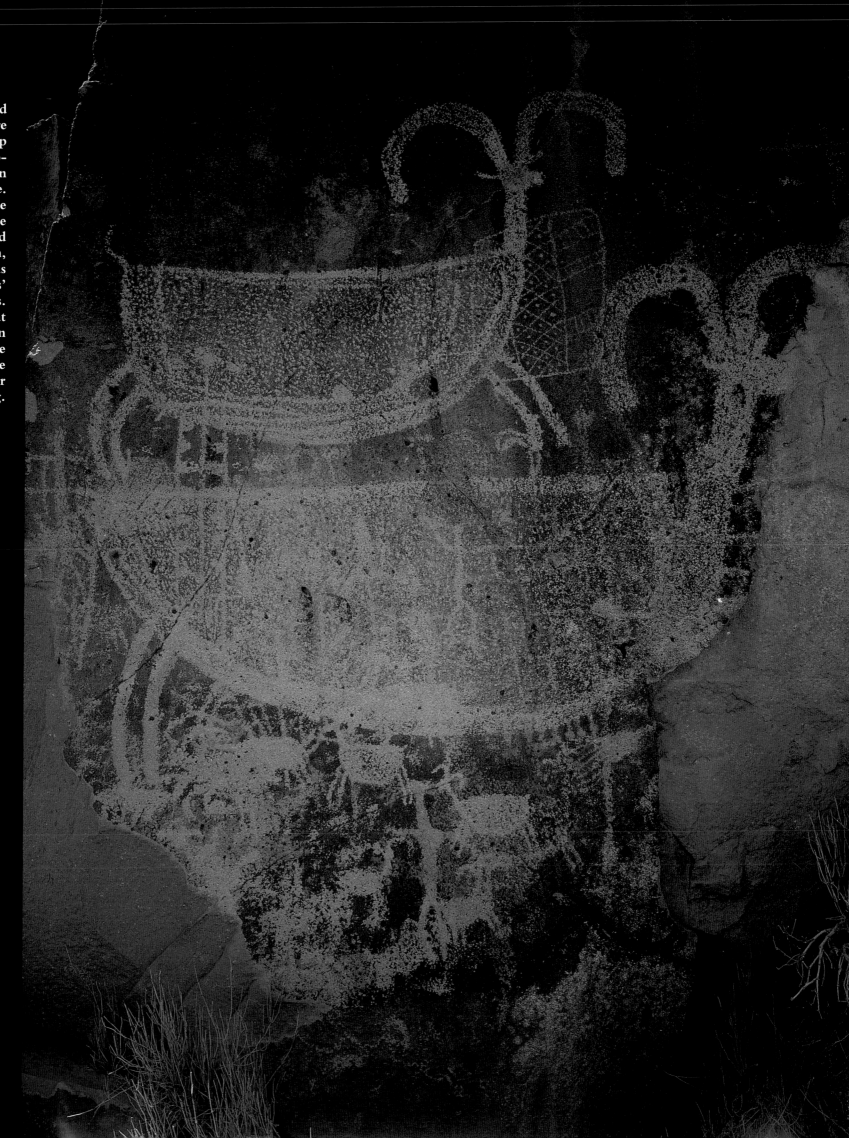

Large boat-shaped Coso Range sheep are superimposed on top of smaller sheep petroglyphs and shaman figures in a similar style. Ethnographically, the Numic-speaking people in this area associated bighorn sheep with rain, and sheep functioned as the rain shamans' specialized helpers. Petroglyphs suggest that this role may have been carried over from the prehistoric past. The larger sheep is over two meters long.

Insect-like stick figures and enigmatic forms pecked on an outcrop near the White Mountain Range in the western Great Basin near Chalfant, California.

Coso Range shamanic figures pecked over small sheep. Differences in the amount of patina and superimposition distinguish newer from older figures.

A patterned-bodied shamanic figure from the Coso Range wears a fringed garment. The face of this figure is abstracted into a set of concentric circles. He is holding weapons and is flanked by lizards and a snake, possibly his spirit helpers.

Green and orange lichen obscure the petroglyphs on this basalt rock face in the Coso Range, but a shaman figure with short arms and over-sized hands remains visible. The skeletonized body pattern reminiscent of ribs is commonly portrayed on shamanistic figures and costumes. This practice springs from ancient traditions and reaches far beyond the North American continent. Among other things, skeletonization represents the shaman's symbolic death and rebirth to a higher order of consciousness.

Great Basin Curvilinear Abstract style petroglyphs and stick figures cover a boulder face near Chalfant, California. The White Mountains define the distant skyline. Petroglyphs similar to these are thought to have been made possibly over a several thousand year period by hunter-gatherers throughout the Great Basin and adjacent parts of the West.

Petroglyph panels near Chalfant, California display round shield-like designs and a wide variety of abstract patterns. Bisected horseshoe-shaped elements or vulvaform designs are female fertility symbols. The light patina on all of these petroglyphs suggests that they are not of great antiquity and that they are the work of Numic speaking peoples after A. D. 1200.

Herring bone patterns and circle motifs painted in red, Cima Dome, Mohave Desert National Preserve, California.

Short-legged animals and sunbursts are among the designs covering the rocks in Grapevine Canyon, Nevada. A curved line pecked into this rock face echoes the form of the stream in the background.

(Preceding pages) Pecked into a basalt outcrop, Great Basin Abstract motifs in California's Mohave Desert feature circles, wavy lines, agglomerated curvilinear patterns, sets of vertical lines, and grid patterns. A small animal and stick figure humans are also present.

Geometric abstract petroglyph patterns are closely massed on this darkly patinated rock in the Newberry Mountains, Nevada. These Great Basin Abstract style motifs consist of rakes, lines of dots, rectilinear squiggles, diamond chains, and decorative squares. Superimpositions and contrasts in patina indicate that figures were added to the rock from time to time during prehistory.

Bold rectilinear abstract designs include
square grids, a barred circular motif, and
other patterns, Mohave Desert, California.

Herring bone patterns and circle motifs painted in red, Cima Dome, Mohave Desert National Preserve, California.

Petroglyphs in Fremont Indian
State Park in Clear Creek Canyon
of west–central Utah feature large
shamanic Fremont anthropomorphs
with horned headdresses along
with bighorn sheep, zigzags, circular
patterns, and random dots. The
designs are carved into soft volcanic
tuff. Estimated dates range between
the late 800s and ca. 1250 A.D.
The Fremont people were village
dwellers with a mixed subsistence
economy in which horticulture
played a variable role.

Miscellaneous petroglyphs at Parowan Gap, in southwestern Utah consist of serpentine animals, ticked lines, and variations on the circle motif, including sunbursts. Fremont farmers, and hunter-gatherers may have contributed to the designs at this site over a period of time.

Petroglyphs, including a horned stick figure, on a basalt bluff, Warner Valley, Oregon.

Unidentifiable plant-like forms comprised of bisected circles are partially enclosed by lines of dots on a volcanic bluff, Warner Valley, Oregon.

GREEN RIVER

THE Green River heads in west central Wyoming south of the Wind River Range. To the east across the continental divide, in the Wind River Valley and the Bighorn Basin, are distinctive petroglyphs that delineate by means of lines and circles human figures and bird-like forms that comprise the Dinwoody or Interior Line style. The majority of these are believed to have been made between one and three thousand years ago by Archaic residents of the area, and stylistic overlaps with rock art in the northern Green River drainage occur.

The Green River is the Colorado's largest tributary, a river that is actually longer than the Colorado itself before the two combine. From its beginnings in Wyoming, its waters snake south through the western edge of the High Plains into the plateaus of eastern Utah. Here the river and its side drainages have sculpted a dramatic series of canyons and tablelands through the colorful, deeply layered sedimentary rocks of the Colorado Plateau. In east central Utah, its greenish waters, filled with sediment, join the Colorado River and double its flow.

The higher plateaus are dotted with subalpine forests, but the middle elevations, dominated by pinyon, juniper, and sagebrush are ultimately more livable. The pinyon/juniper zone, along with the slightly lower grasslands where saltbush and rice grass flourish, would have been rich in plant resources for foragers of the natural seasonal harvest. By around 6000 B.C. hunting-gathering bands of the Western Archaic tradition were established in this rugged landscape. Dry caves in the massive sandstone formations of the Colorado Plateau often served as temporary campsites. In these caves, artifacts and refuse have been well preserved, remains that have provided good records of hunter-gatherer life. Painted pebbles, split-twig figurines, and unbaked clay figurines supplement the graphic art on the sandstone walls. The abundant rock art in the area is often a legacy of ancient shamanistic traditions, and is the most immediate and eloquent evidence of the presence of these early peoples.

In the same region, for eight or nine hundred years or so during the late prehistoric period, farming peoples known as the Fremont grew corn, beans, and squash and lived in small pit-house villages or in stone masonry dwellings. They, too, continued the tradition of shamanism and left documents of these rituals carved and painted on stone in the canyon labyrinths. Typically, Fremont rock art consists of rows of figures in frontal view, often with ceremonial attire and holding ritual objects.

Efforts to farm in these cold uplands, however, were short-lived relative to the enduring character of the hunter-gatherer life-style. Around A. D. 1300 the Fremont culture vanished, to be replaced by the ancestors of the Utes who continued the Archaic way of life. Today the Utes continue to live on tribal lands on the plateaus of the Green River drainage.

Wind River figures with big heads and short bodies combine human and avian characteristics and perhaps represent owl shamans. Some have large eyes as well.

Bird shamans and owl figures characterize the Dinwoody Interior Line style found in the Wind River Range, Wyoming. Interior designs include small circles, wavy lines, dots, and elements in which parallel lines are emphasized. Most of the petroglyphs in the Dinwoody Tradition are believed to have been made by hunter-gatherers between 1000 and 3000 years ago.

Interior-line style owls appear to ascend
this lichen-covered sandstone wall in
the Wind River Range, Wyoming.

In the Dinwoody Tradition,
round-eyed shamanic figures are
pecked on a heavily weathered
boulder in the Wind River Range.

Classic Vernal style Fremont petroglyphs in northeastern Utah are noteworthy for their scale and complexity. Life-size elaborately attired ceremonial figures are pecked in a row across the base of a towering sandstone cliff in Dry Fork Canyon. They all have facial features, and they wear complicated headgear, heavy necklaces, armbands, and sashes. In their hands they hold flayed heads. Estimated dates for the Classic Vernal style range from A.D. 600 to 1000.

In this Classic Vernal style panel in the Dry Fork valley, the center figure is shown with enormous over-sized feet and a flayed head with face and neck intact dangles from his elbow. Another is visible at the extreme right. Traces of red paint here and there indicate that these figures were once more extensively painted.

Carefully delineated giant lizards
pecked on sandstone in Dinosaur
National Monument are probably the
work of Fremont artists, although the
lizard is normally not found in
Fremont styles.

(Preceding pages) The face of a high sandstone
bluff near a creek junction in central Utah is covered with many layers of petroglyphs. Shamanic
and fertility themes prevail. Many of the animals
lack counterparts in the natural world, although
owls, sheep, and deer are clearly present. A huge
rainbow is among the latest figures pecked into
this cliff face. This spot may have been a ceremonial or ritual retreat for many centuries. The
petroglyphs are believed to pre-date A. D. 1200.

Broad-shouldered Classic Vernal style figures in Dinosaur National Monument, Utah, holding shields. The bison are later additions.

Communicating a sense of the supernatural through millennia, a Barrier Canyon Style shaman flanked by spirit helpers or guardian deities seems to hover on a yellow cliff face in central Utah.

Photo by Marc Muench

A row of Fremont petroglyphs pecked as a group on a sandstone slab in Nine Mile Canyon, Utah, includes big-horn sheep, figurine-like anthropomorphs, a snake, scorpion, and shield-bearer.

A petroglyph panel crowded with many designs near the Green River in central Utah was the site of repeated visitation. A row of short-armed anthropomorphs, with fingers splayed, appears to have been conceived of as a group. Stylistic affiliations suggest that these anthropomorphs pre-date the Fremont of this area. Many of the abstract elements appear to be later additions.

A unified scene dominated by a central horned shaman and a line of mountain sheep occupies a sandstone overhang in Nine Mile Canyon, Utah. Below hunters with bows and arrows engage in pursuit of a herd in which the sheep are linked to each other by lines that extend from their noses. The significance of the small shield bearer in the center of the panel is unclear. Dates for this petroglyph composition are estimated on the basis of the Fremont occupation in the northern San Rafael region, A. D. 700-1250.

Barrier Canyon "Great Gallery"
Painted anthropomorphs in
Canyonlands National Park

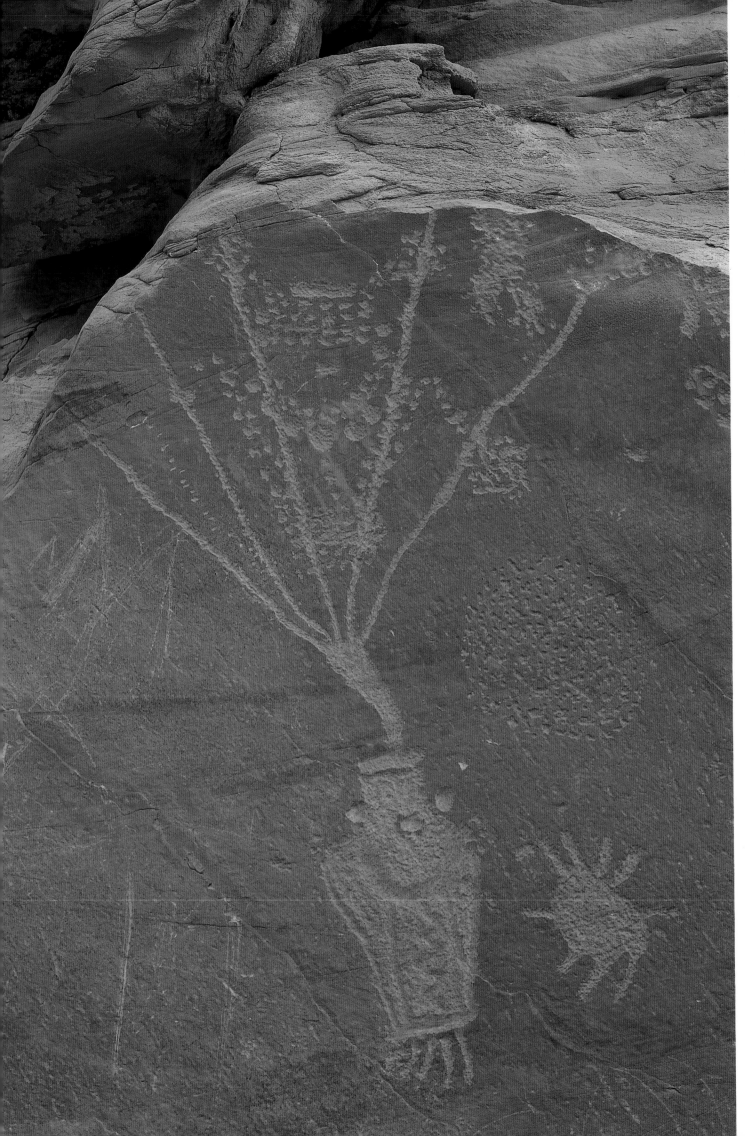

Traces of Fremont designs on this sandstone face in Dinosaur National Monument include beaded necklaces and other suggestions of shamanic attire. Superimposed over these are five long lines that radiate from the head of a small armless anthropomorphic form. This figure also wears a necklace and other decorations.

From the San Rafael region, a panel of elongated Barrier Canyon style figures painted in dark red comprise a shamanic scene. The anthropomorphs are accompanied by delicately rendered, detailed animals. These animals, as well as the plants pictured, may represent spirit helpers. Transformational themes in this group include animals holding staffs like humans and the left-hand shaman with wings. As in other examples, a combination of man and bird features suggests ascent to the celestial realm.

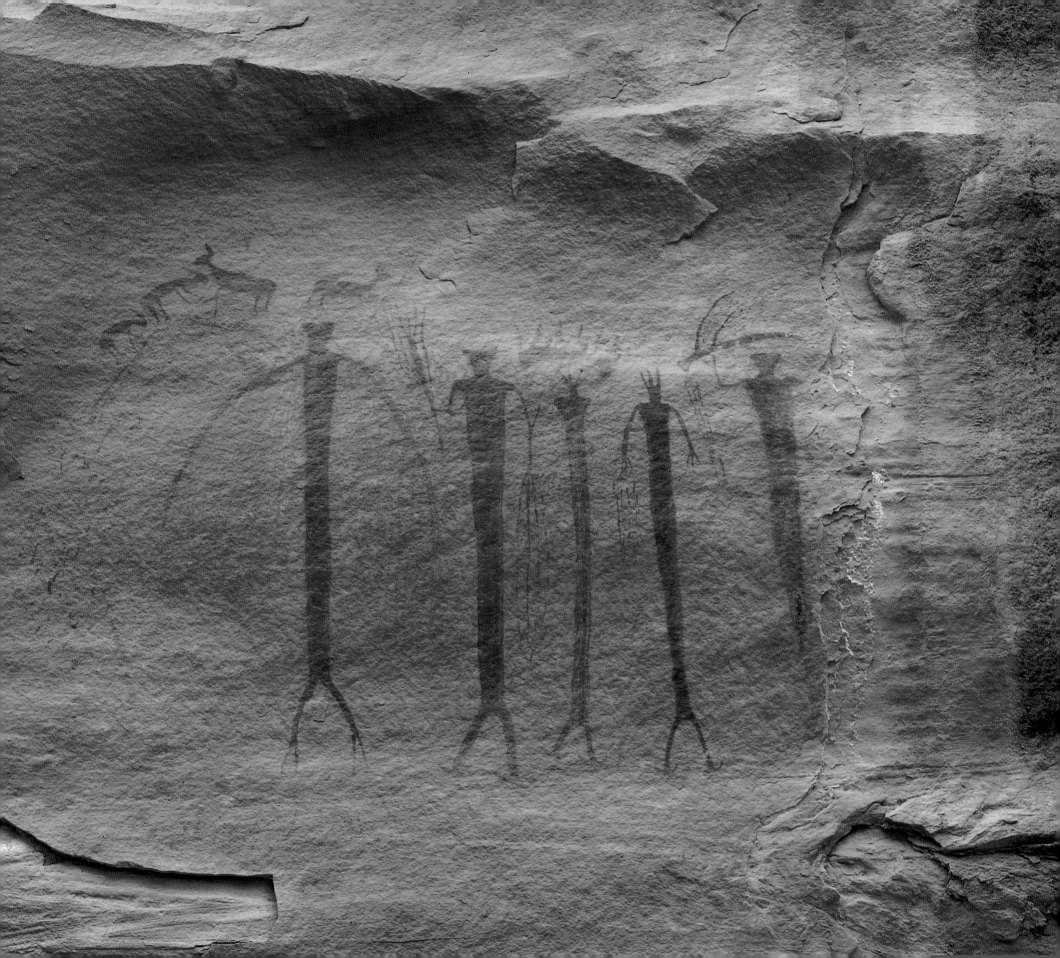

Dark ghost-like Barrier Canyon style shamanic forms cluster around an ethereal central anthropomorph over two meters tall with staring eyes. An unusual feature of this figure is the fact that it was created by a spray painting technique that effectively contributes to its appearance of insubstantiality. The group as a whole seems to define a three dimensional space on this sandstone surface.

COLORADO RIVER

THE 1700 mile long Colorado River is truly the "Mother Ditch," the Acequia Madre, of southwestern rivers, collecting as it does the waters from all other major rivers that traverse the Southwest landscape west of the Continental Divide. The Colorado itself has its origins in the melting snows of the Rocky Mountains and ultimately ends in a muddy delta, where it disperses its accumulated load into the Gulf of California. The middle of its journey, however, is through the high Colorado Plateau where in the course of eons it has carved formidable and twisted canyons through sedimentary layers of purple, red, and yellow to expose a slice of geologic time. In the Grand Canyon its watery edge has cut down into the Pre-cambrian schists and granites formed before life on earth began.

It is not surprising that the Grand Canyon is an important part of the sacred landscape of native peoples who have lived and who continue to live on the Colorado Plateau. For the Hopis it is their place of origin, the Sipapu, where they emerged from the Underworld, and the place to which the dead return. Likewise the Zunis hold memories of shrines and descriptions of sacred localities in the canyon's depths.

Although a few western Anasazi lived for a time in the Canyon bottom where the environment is often hot and hostile, traces of human prehistory in the Colorado River drainage are usually found on the upland mesas and plateaus and in the well watered side canyons of tributary drainages. The rock art and other archaeological remains tell much the same story throughout the Colorado Plateau. For several thousand years hunter-gatherers made their seasonal rounds leaving evidence of their campsites in the many available rock shelters and on the mesa tops and canyon bottoms. Barrier Canyon style paintings in eastern Utah and petroglyphs in Glen Canyon, now flooded by Glen Canyon Dam, are visual documents of their cosmologies and shamanistic practices. Perhaps their most spectacular statements are to be found in rock shelters in the western Grand Canyon of Arizona where detailed paintings of supernatural figures are packed into tight compositions.

The Anasazi that followed for over 1500 years or more left artifacts of their history. Deep rock shelters formed by wind and water in the Navajo sandstone preserved their storage cists, cliff dwellings, pottery, baskets, sandals, and of course their rock art. Rock paintings of the Anasazi also include numerous examples of their hand prints. The rock art of the Anasazi in the Colorado drainage varied according to cultural changes through time and by region, and many of the examples that follow are on the northern and western peripheries of the Anasazi domain.

As along the Green River, so too along the Colorado, during the 13th century, the farming Anasazi disappeared to be replaced by hunter-gatherers once again. In historical times, the Utes have also left a record on the rocks, one that includes horses and artifacts from a rapidly changing world.

This large shield-bearer in white, red, and gray is widely known as "The All American Man." It is superimposed on top of faded handprints from an earlier time. Recent radio-carbon dates of the paint suggest that the shield-bearer was painted in the fourteenth century. Canyonlands National Park, Utah.

Anasazi cliff dwellings such as Inscription House in northern Arizona were built within sandstone alcoves in the canyons of the Kayenta region between A. D. 1250 and 1300.

(Preceding pages) The active stances of these combative figures from Indian Creek Canyon in Utah is unusual. Both carry weapons in their left hands. Their hair and headdress styles suggest a late Basketmaker date between A.D. 400 – 600.

A row of Anasazi hands from Natural Bridges National Monument looks freshly printed.

Paintings in various shades of white form a mural across a smooth sandstone face in Canyonlands National Park, Utah.

A line of thirteen large elaborate painted human figures in an inconspicuous alcove in Canyonlands National Park, Utah. This site is called the "Thirteen Faces." Figurine-like, these anthropomorphic forms lack arms and legs, but display carefully delineated faces, necklaces, earrings, and body paint, and they appear to wear kilts. In shape and detail they closely resemble Fremont clay figurines that may date as late as A.D. 1250, but they often occur near Anasazi structures. Regardless of who painted them, they are part of the Fremont art tradition and seem to signify a complex ideological interaction between the Fremont and Anasazi populations in southeastern Utah.

more extensive group painted
several thousand years ago.

(Preceding pages) A large panel of nineteenth century Ute petroglyphs has been pecked on top of prehistoric rock art at Newspaper Rock State Park along Indian Creek, Utah. The Ute images include horseback riders, people with fringed leggings, bison, hides or animal pelts, and innumerable copies of the older designs. Bear paws are a prominent motif as are mountain sheep and deer. The spoked circle may represent a wagon wheel.

Known as "The Four Faces," these Canyonlands paintings in red, white, and blue-green depict female figures comparable to those represented by clay Fremont figurines. The hair is tied in "bobs" at either side of the face, and their slit eyes are like the clay "coffee bean" eyes of figurines. Each of the three in red wears a necklace with a single stone.

The "Five Faces" fill space framed by black water streaks in a sandstone alcove. A male figure with a bandelier across the chest is bordered on each side by two females with hair-bobs. At this site, the sandstone has been smoothed in preparation for painting the facial region.

Most of these petroglyphs at Atlatl Rock, Valley of Fire State Park, Nevada are probably attributable to the Anasazi of the Virgin Branch (A. D. 1000 to ca. 1125). The atlatl and spear at the top of the panel are earlier. The outlined cross is not specific to any style and is widely distributed throughout the American West and northern Mexico.

An Anasazi storage room near Kachina
Bridge in Natural Bridges National
Monument with Fremont style paintings on its walls. Hand prints and
simple painted designs are visible
on the mud-streaked sandstone that
forms the back wall of the alcove.

In the Paria River, a tumbled boulder bearing petroglyphs rests precariously on a talus slope. Among the figures, now upside-down, can be seen hands and various anthropomorphs, including a shield-bearer.

Pecked on sandstone, Abajo-LaSal style bighorn sheep with exaggerated necks, Indian Creek Canyon, Utah.

Rabbit tracks, animals, and simple human figures share a sandstone wall with lichens and a water streak in Indian Creek Canyon, Utah. The petroglyphs are Abajo-LaSal style Anasazi, and they were made prior to A. D. 900.

These Fremont style elements from Indian Creek Canyon include figurine-shaped anthropomorphic forms, sheep, and zigzags that may represent snakes or lightning. A small fluteplayer is visible near the left-hand anthropomorph.

Parade of bighorn sheep pecked through black patina on sandstone, Indian Creek Canyon, Utah.

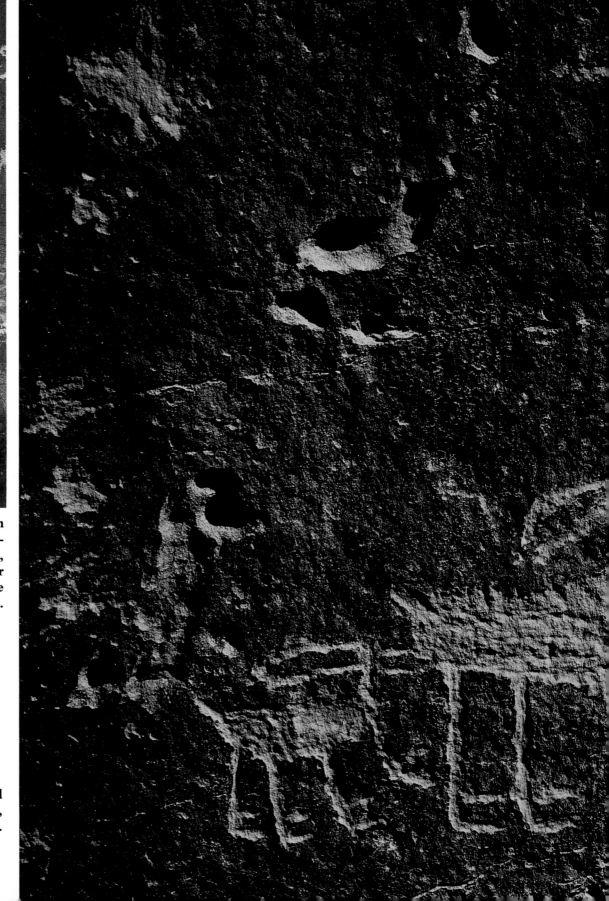

This rock shelter includes life-sized paintings of supernaturals and/or shamans painted in red, white, orange, and green. In this group perhaps we are viewing a male shaman flanked by spirits. The figure on the left has a complex interior pattern including the possible depiction of ribs. There is abundant evidence that the wall was painted repeatedly, probably in connection with a number of different ritual events. Arms of an earlier large figure are visible behind the central anthropomorph.

The setting sun illuminates a sandstone rock shelter on the Arizona Strip filled with paintings of elongated anthropomorphic forms. The paintings were made by hunter-gatherer artists more than 2000 years ago.

Basketmaker paintings in the Arizona Strip region feature flat bucket-shaped heads, slit eyes, and necklaces. Some have their hair tied in "bobs" on either side of the head. Like their San Juan cousins, these shaman figures are often phallic and shown with drooping hands and feet.

Colorado River at dawn, Toroweap, Grand Canyon National Park.

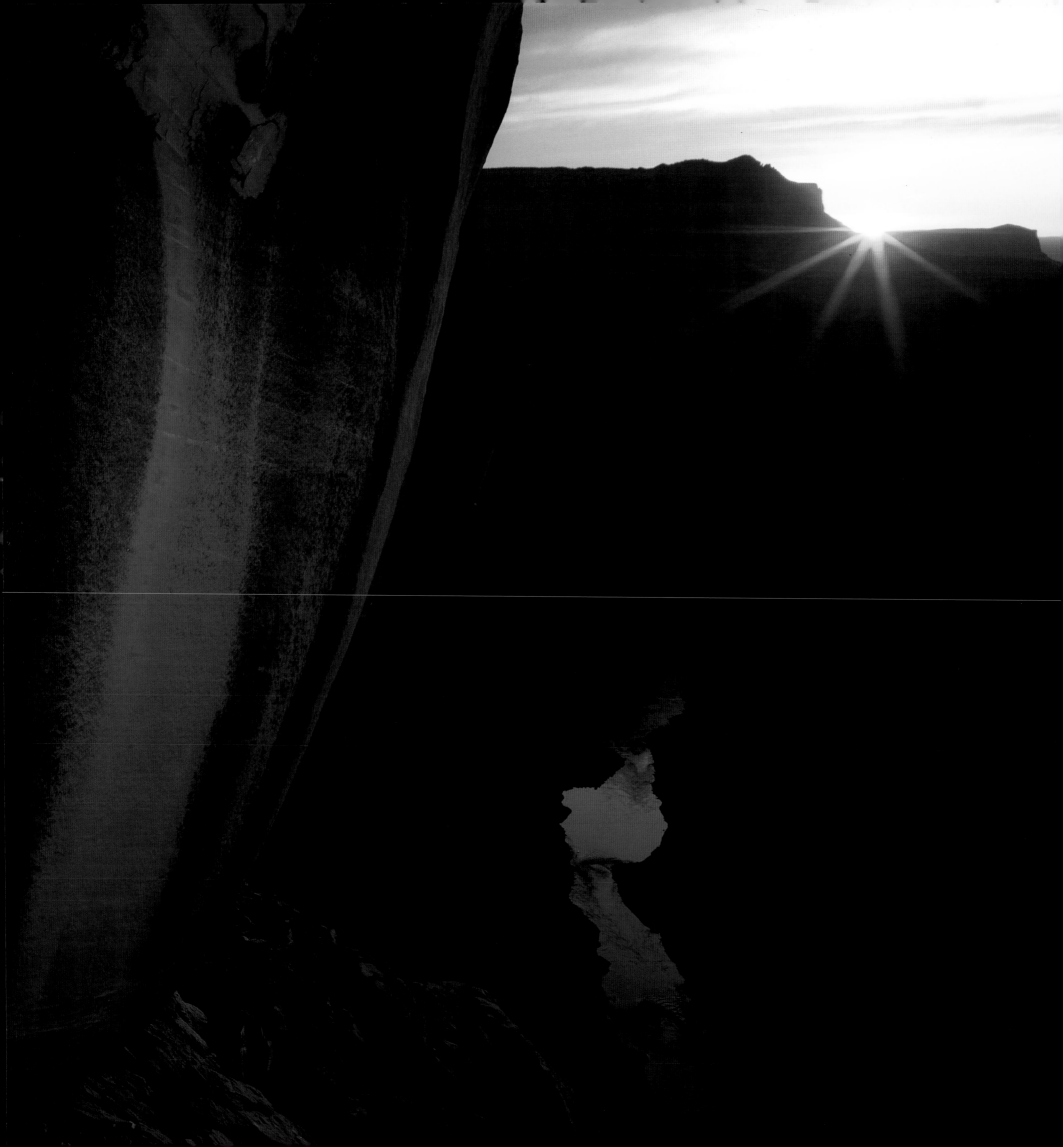

LITTLE COLORADO RIVER

RIVERS and streams that drain the high Mogollon Rim country in east central Arizona combine with the Rio Puerco and Zuni River which rise in low mountains and mesas near the Continental Divide in New Mexico to form the Little Colorado. Trending in a northwest direction, this network of creeks and washes carves into low relief an arid landscape exposing colorful sedimentary beds. The heart of the Little Colorado drainage includes Petrified Forest and the Painted Desert. Only in the final miles of its course does the Little Colorado descend to the entrenched canyon system of the Colorado River itself.

The area embraces the ancestral sites of the Western Pueblo peoples, the Hopi and Zuni, who maintain clan rights to specific locations and an active relationship with shrines and places of mythological importance in the regions beyond their villages.

Prehistoric occupation of the Little Colorado region dates back to well before the first Basketmakers around 2000 years ago. Afterwards, this area sustained a small farming population that substantially increased after A.D. 1300 when pueblo immigrants from the north moved into the region and were assimilated by the resident Anasazi. Petroglyphs illustrated here are largely the work of Anasazi between A.D. 1000 and 1300. From near Zuni, on the other hand, are paintings of kachinas made at intervals during the 20th century.

Further west in the vicinity of Wupatki and Sunset Crater, the archaeological record of the farming peoples indicates that culturally this was a distinct group, known to archaeologists as the Sinagua. Their rock art is similar, although they seem to have placed an even greater emphasis on the textile designs that are so frequently encountered in Little Colorado River rock art made between approximately A.D. 1050 and 1300.

In this painting the Zuni Cow Kachina is epresented with bulging eyes and with a hand print on the face of the mask.

A row of life-size 20th century kachina masks painted in a rock shelter near Zuni Pueblo in western New Mexico. These masked supernaturals are associated with clouds and rain, but assume individual and diverse personalities. From left to right are Atoshle, a male Scare Kachina; a Comanche dancer; Hehea, the Blunderer; and the Zuni Shalako.

Rock art along this sandstone ledge offers contrasting views of Pueblo styles and iconography across the centuries. To the left are contemporary paintings of kachina masks. To the right is a panel of petroglyphs pecked around 800 years ago by Zuni ancestors. Their original meanings have been lost over time, but contemporary Zunis view these as an important part of their mythic past. They say that stick figures and lizard-like men depict man at the "time of the beginning" before he was "finished" or completely human. Spirals such as these are sometimes considered to be spiritual "maps" representing the "journey to the center," or to Zuni itself.

Historic Pueblo petroglyphs on sandstone
from near Zuni, New Mexico. A sun face,
an animal with a heartline, and a group
of ceremonial participants, possibly
representing the Mudhead Clowns.

A large human figure and fine rectilinear scroll designs appear to be the work of different Anasazi artisans, probably between A. D. 1100–1300. They are located near a cave entrance in Petrified Forest National Park, Arizona.

Pecked by Anasazi through dark patina on a sandstone rock face, this bold composite animal combines feline paws and tail with the horns of a mountain sheep, Petrified Forest National Park.

Anasazi designs cut into a smooth boulder face in Petrified Forest National Park create an intricate pattern. Visible in this photograph are geometric pottery motifs, zigzags and snakes, a spiral and miscellaneous life forms. A line of bear tracks extends from the upper left to lower right. Stylistic comparisons suggest dates between A.D. 1000 and 1300 for these petroglyphs.

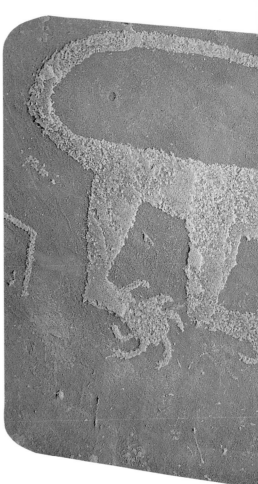

A yowling cat pecked on sandstone is distinguished by its long tail that curves over its back and its long curved claws. In style it is typical of the late Anasazi occupation in the Petrified Forest region between A. D. 1250 and 1400.

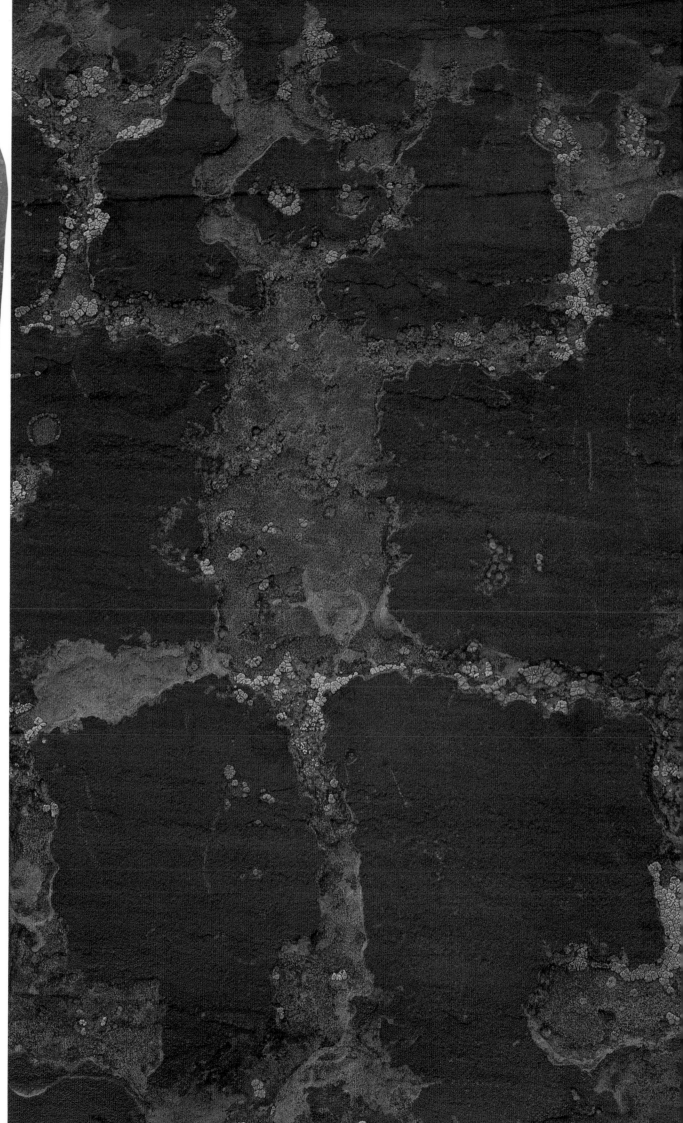

Anasazi lizard-man.
Estimated dates range
between A. D. 1000
and 1300. Petrified
Natural Forest.

Spirals on sandstone in Wupatki National Monument evoke Hopi and Zuni folktales of "finding the Center," of spiraling inward in the search for place. Lines extending from the outer lines of the spirals have figures on them, seemingly representing those embarking on this journey. Perhaps clans or culture heroes are depicted as travelers by the artists that pecked these figures sometime between A. D. 1000 and 1225.

A snake, long-necked anthropomorphic forms, and a sunburst pattern a sandstone wall above an aperture that frames the San Francisco Peaks in northern Arizona. These figures were made around a thousand years ago by regional farmers who shared Anasazi, Sinagua, and Cohonino cultural characteristics.

Simple prehistoric
images are visible
on a small rock face
slightly darkened with
patina below a heavily
eroded sandstone wall.
Among these a human
figure, a cat, bird, and
snake are distinguishable.
On the left is a seated
fluteplayer, and in the
center is another, lying
on his back.

On an exposed edge
of a boulder, a spiral
with a ticked edge may
represent the sun, Wupatki
National Monument,
Arizona, A. D. 1000
to 1225.

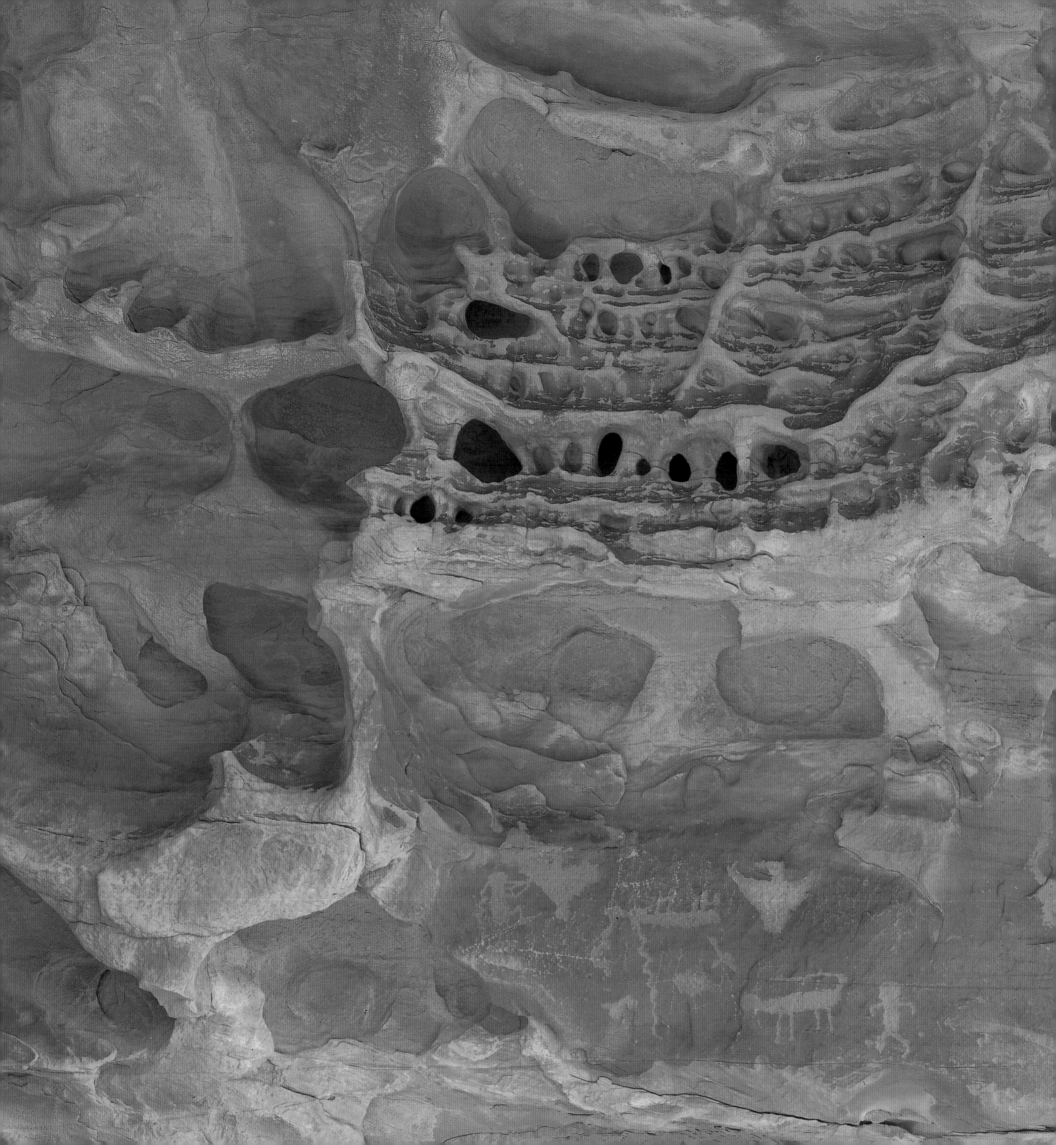

SAN JUAN RIVER

IN THE snowy heights of the San Juan Mountains in southwestern Colorado are the headwaters of the San Juan River, a major Colorado River tributary. The San Juan quickly ceases to be a mountain stream on its southwestern trajectory into New Mexico. There it takes on the character of a muddy desert flow, winding first through forested canyon uplands, then progressing downward through open high desert grasslands and scrub past Shiprock and the Four Corners. Once in Utah, the river begins its long approach to the Colorado itself, via an entrenched, meandering course through spectacular canyons. Throughout its course, side canyons lead back from the river to well-watered canyon heads and higher mesas covered with pinyon and juniper where Anasazi farmers could grow crops and establish village life.

Some time after 800 B.C. the San Juan drainage became home to the first Anasazi Basketmaker farmers whose ancestors may have been the preceding hunter-gatherers of the area. The farming culture persisted and diversified in the San Juan drainage, and three major divisions are recognized by archaeologists: the Mesa Verde, Chaco, and the Kayenta. By A. D. 1300 the entire San Juan region, for a variety of reasons not yet clearly understood, was abandoned by the Anasazi. Cliff dwellings and storage rooms, the standing walls of Chaco ruins, pottery, stone tools, and rock art are evidence of their presence.

Along the lower San Juan and in its side drainages, including Chinle Wash and Canyon de Chelly, Basketmaker rock art is the most distinctive. Its primary focus is the big broad-shouldered shamanic figure with necklaces and crescent-shaped headdresses. Painted handprints, birds, spears and spear throwers (otherwise known as *atlatls*), yucca plants, medicine bags, and flayed heads or scalps, are associated elements. Later Anasazi rock art is characterized by simpler figures.

Today, west from Farmington, New Mexico the river is bordered on the south by the Navajo Reservation. The old Navajo country, the Dinetah, is a much smaller region of high mesas dissected by canyons east of Farmington. It is here that Navajo culture took shape in the early 1700s under the stimulus of Pueblo refugees from the Rio Grande. Navajo myths refer to specific landscape localities in the Dinetah, and rock paintings and petroglyphs on sandstone walls picture supernaturals, shields, clouds, corn, and animals of symbolic importance. Many of these sites show evidence of frequent visitation and may have functioned as shrines and places of power.

Stick figures, a hand, and a wavy line are visible in this detailed view of an extensive petroglyph panel at Pictograph Point in Mesa Verde National Park, Colorado. The figures are pecked on heavily patinated sandstone and were made by Anasazi Pueblo farmers of the Mesa Verde between A. D. 1050 and 1280.

A view through an Anasazi T-shaped doorway, Long House Ruin, Wetherill Mesa, Mesa Verde National Park, Colorado.

This Navajo *ye'i*, or supernatural, known as "the god of harvest, god of plenty, god of mist" holds a staff, or digging stick, and wears mountain sheep horns and a feathered hump that contains seeds and moisture. This supernatural is important today in the Night Chant ceremony.

Rock paintings in white clays and red mineral pigments by Anasazi Basketmakers, Canyon de Chelly, Arizona. Estimated dates fall between 200 B. C. and A. D. 500. The Basketmakers were the first farmers on the Colorado Plateau, and their prolific rock art tells us that their religion was shamanic in focus. Large static figures with tall head-dresses, necklaces, and drooping hands and feet are typical of early Basketmaker rock art throughout the lower San Juan region. The elements extending from the left ear may symbolize a shaman's supernatural hearing capacities.

A late Basketmaker painting in Canyon de Chelly of an anthropomorph, possibly a shaman. The lines emanating from his head are suggestive of his supernatural powers, and the smaller red figures could be spirit helpers, A. D. 400–600.

In Canyon de Chelly, these small late Basketmaker fluteplayers in red play their music under rainbows. Fluteplayers, fertility, warmth, and moisture are linked concepts in the Pueblo world even today. These early fluteplayers are wearing headdresses with upright feathers and white sashes are indicated at their waists. Actual flutes made of boxelder wood and decorated with small brightly colored bird feathers have been found in the nearby dry caves, once lived in by these late Basketmaker people. Lending scale to this photo is a faint white handprint, visible between the fluteplayers.

In this sandstone alcove south of the San Juan River in northern Arizona, are square-shouldered shamanic anthropomorphs and handprints left by Basketmakers around 2000 years ago. In the A.D. 1200s the Anasazi built their houses of rock and mud below the paintings of their Basketmaker ancestors.

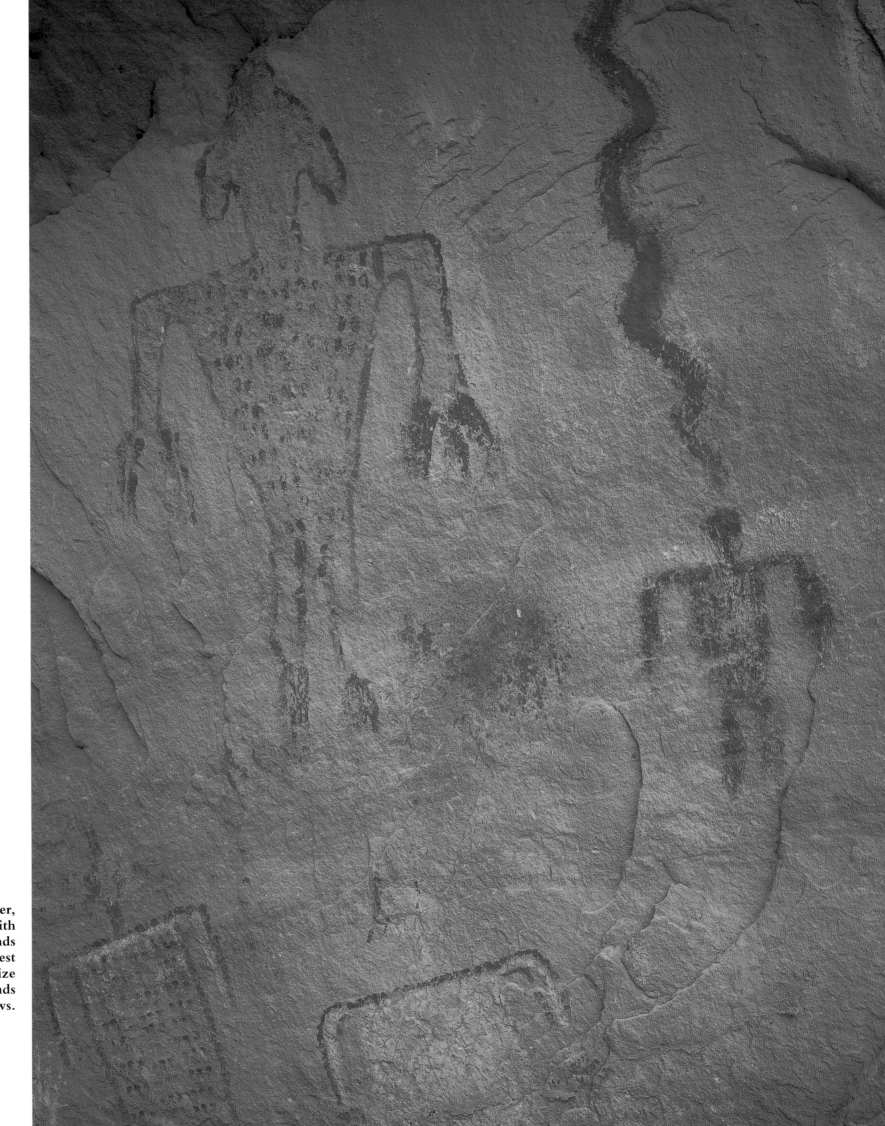

In the same rock shelter, this green shaman with dots on his body stands out from the rest through his large size and color. His hands and feet are like claws.

Large white shields of different designs painted above a doorway and walled sandstone ledge in Grand Gulch. The rock art and the masonry were made by the last Anasazi to inhabit these canyons in the 1200s. A dark red hand print is faintly visible at the bottom right of the left-hand shield. It is possible that these shield motifs were painted as a form of protective magic at these late, seemingly defensive sites. By A.D. 1300 the Anasazi had migrated out of the San Juan drainage where their ancestral roots reached back more than 1500 years.

In the Lukachukai region, on a sandstone wall darkened with desert varnish, a rich pattern of images includes arms and hands and square-bodied Anasazi bighorn sheep superimposed by a "waving" figure. Light-colored lines and areas in the pecking suggest historic defacement. The "waving" figure also appears to be recent or subject to historic period repecking.

Multi-colored lichen patterns cover sandstone ledges and fallen slabs in front of an image-filled Grand Gulch alcove. The Anasazi petroglyphs visible in the background include a long snake and long-legged birds and most notably tall figures with large heads that seem to wave at passersby.

A depiction of a life-sized flayed head occurs as an isolated figure in a rock shelter above other Basketmaker paintings in Grand Gulch. The face is brightly painted in yellow and green stripes and framed by red hair. A loop for carrying is faintly visible on top. As in the Fremont culture, skins like this are thought to have been used as fetishes or power objects. Estimated dates range from 200 B.C. to A.D. 500.

These weathered but imposing male San Juan Basketmaker shaman figures are part of a larger group seemingly created by one individual. Their broad-shouldered form is classic as are the towering headdresses, ear pieces, and drooping hands and feet. The individual on the right with a large head holds in the left hand a disembodied head surmounted by a stack of crescents. The feet have claws and look more animal than human. The figures approximate a meter in height. San Juan River, Utah, 200 B. C. - A. D. 400.

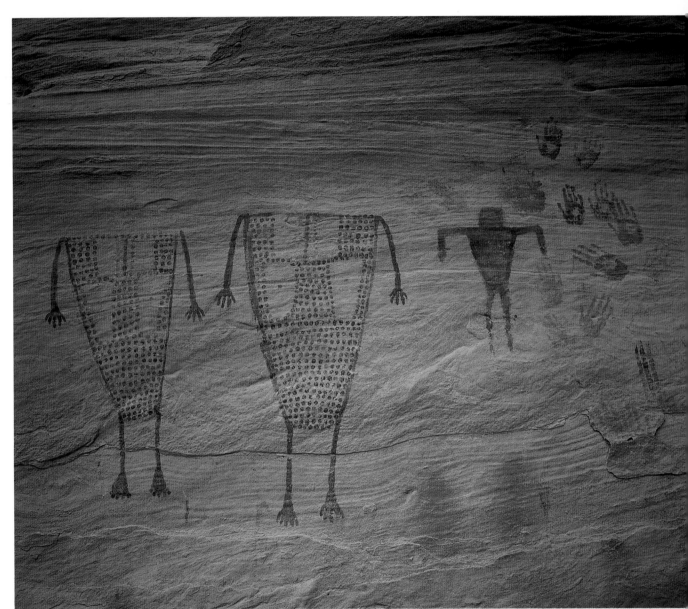

Large red Basketmaker figures with bodies carefully filled with red dots. Traces of heads are faintly visible. A rather abstract designation of breasts indicates that these are female figures. Providing scale, to the right, handprints cluster near a smaller anthropomorph. Grand Gulch, Utah, 200 B. C. to A. D. 400.

Walls of a ruin tucked beneath an overhang in a Cedar Mesa canyon. The
original mud plaster is still intact. The
wide band of white with two triangles
suspended below and a continuous row
of dots at the upper edge is an unusual
example of Anasazi architectural
painted decoration. Perhaps other
walls, now denuded of their plaster,
were once similarly enhanced.

Spirals, a lizard, bird, human figure, and various animals form a tight group of Anasazi petroglyphs on the sandstone cliffs behind ruins at Chaco Canyon National Historic Park, New Mexico. Various bear or human tracks are also visible. A lack of adherence to natural models is apparent in the bird with antlers. The petroglyphs are thought to date between A. D. 1000 and 1200.

For at least 1500 years a bird-headed stick figure, an undistinguished anthropomorph, and an elongated fluteplayer have enhanced this Cedar Mesa sandstone slab.

A composite painting on sandstone, Chinle Wash, Utah. Basketmaker anthropomorphs and a set of white handprints decorated this cliff face for possibly over a thousand years before thirteenth century Anasazis painted the red and white circular shield over the largest of the Basketmaker figures. The stenciled handprint was also added at this time.

Rock faces blackened by desert varnish appealed to late Basketmaker petroglyph artists of the San Juan region. A duck-headed shaman pecked through blue-black patina vividly contrasts with the surrounding surface. Estimated dates for this figure fall between A. D. 200 and 600.

Early Anasazi petroglyphs, probably late Basketmaker in age, cluster on this expansive smooth face of a giant sandstone slab in Monument Valley, Utah. Two large projectiles pierce the shoulders of a broad shouldered figure above a fluteplayer. Unusual oval-bodied figures may depict females, and a woman with hair whorls seems to be giving birth in the lower panel on the right.

Fertility is a major theme in Anasazi rock art. From Cedar Mesa we see a time sequence represented in two scenes: on the left, a copulating couple, and on the right, the birth of a baby. Above the female giving birth is the head of a snake that continues off to the right. The head of the snake is pecked around a hole in the rock.

Bird shamans dominate this early Anasazi panel near John's Canyon at the foot of Cedar Mesa. The left-hand figure has bird-like three digit hands and feet as well as a bird for a head. Snakes, animals, and miscellaneous human figures make up the rest of the figures pecked on this rock face.

San Juan Basketmaker petroglyphs on Cedar Mesa include themes of fertility, bird-headed shamans, and projectiles. Hand-holding pairs, stick figures, simple snakes, animal tracks, and birds by themselves are also representative of late Basketmaker and early Pueblo work.

GILA RIVER

AT HEIGHTS of 10,000 feet in the Mogollon Mountains of southwestern New Mexico, not far from Mimbres country, the Gila River begins its long course westward across southern Arizona to join the Colorado at the California border. Through most of its course it is a desert river moving through a landscape characterized by isolated ranges alternating with wide desert basins. In south central Arizona it crosses the semi-arid Lower Sonoran Desert characterized by giant saguaro cacti, as well as by creosote bush, palo verde, ironwood, mesquite, and saltbush. Further west in the Lower Colorado Desert, the elevation drops and the land becomes hotter as one approaches the Colorado River itself. This western region was occupied by pottery-making people who depended primarily on foraging for a living, supplemented with some farming activities.

The Salt and Gila river basins of what is now south-central Arizona are where Hohokam farmers developed their distinctive society between A.D. 500 and 1450. These village dwellers, living in informally arranged brush structures, harnessed the waters of the Gila and the Salt, constructing major canals as part of extensive hydraulic networks to irrigate their crops of corn, beans, squash, and cotton. Ball

courts, and after A. D. 1000 artificial mounds and council or society houses, characterized their larger sites. In the Tucson Basin, lacking major desert rivers with which to irrigate, a regional version of the Hohokam culture developed.

Hohokam art forms included elaborately painted pottery, stone bowls called "censers," figurines, carved stone pallets, shell jewelry, as well as rock art. Surprisingly, Hohokam rock art, largely in the form of petroglyphs, is simple in concept. Spirals and abstract curvilinear designs are the most frequent. Representational forms commonly include lizards and deer, mountain sheep, coyotes, and snakes. The lizard must have been an important symbolic figure in Hohokam religion as it is found represented on ceramics, slate palettes, stone bowls, and carved shell as well as in the rock art. In addition, groups of dancers are sometimes pictured on the rocks, as well as on pottery. The distribution of Hohokam petroglyphs in the landscape is varied, suggesting that the reasons for making them were equally diverse. They are found on rocky buttes, along what seem to be prehistoric trails, in places where wild foods would have been processed, and in rock shelters thought to have been the sites of ritual activities.

A desert bighorn sheep races across a basalt rock face, the Gila River region, Arizona. Dates and cultural affiliations are uncertain, but this petroglyph is probably the work of Hakataya pottery-making people who lived in the Lower Colorado desert between A. D. 300 and 1400.

A Hohokam desert farmer pecked this highly stylized bighorn sheep and abstract design of scrolls, dots, and diamonds on a volcanic escarpment near the Gila River, Arizona. Estimated dates are between A.D. 650-1050.

A Sonoran Desert landscape with yellow brittlebush and Hohokam petroglyphs on black volcanic boulders.

An animal and line of hand-holding stick figures, possibly dancers, made by the Hohokam, in south–central Arizona. The depiction of ceremonial activities such as dancing is rare.

Stick figure lizards, humans, sheep, an outlined cross, and miscellaneous other petroglyphs were probably made by Hohokam farmers of the lower Sonoran desert of Arizona.

Hohokam petroglyphs, Saguaro
National Monument, Arizona.
Above the brittlebush, two stick
figures with horns are visible.

Hohokam petroglyphs, Saguaro National Monument, Arizona. The sun-burst, animal and flower-like patterns are typical Hohokam designs.

Petroglyphs on basalt, Gila River, Arizona.

RIO GRANDE

RISING on the eastern slopes of the San Juan Mountains in southwestern Colorado and ending at the Gulf of Mexico, the Rio Grande is the second longest river in the United States. From the high mountains of Colorado it cuts a series of deep gorges through the pinyon and juniper uplands of northern New Mexico above present-day Albuquerque. At this point the Rio Grande becomes a truly desert river, its muddy water winding south into the Chihuahuan Desert where its tributaries are rough dry arroyos fed only by the torrential rains of summer thunderstorms. At El Paso where it becomes the international boundary between the United States and Mexico, the Rio Grande is scarcely more than a stream that persists into the Big Bend country. Here it is renewed by the Mexican Rio Conchos and the Pecos River of Texas to carry on to the hot humid lowlands of south Texas and the Gulf.

The Rio Grande was the home of numerous peoples and cultures for thousands of years in the prehistoric past, and historically the river has been the stage for dramas of the Spanish conquistadors and the mission period that followed. The varied story of its human history and the cosmologies of its people are found painted and carved in abundance on the rocks throughout its course and in the neighboring desert bolsons.

Some of the most complex and expressive shamanic rock paintings in North America are found in the deep limestone rock shelters on the Rio Grande and near the mouths of the Pecos and Devils Rivers in West Texas and in neighboring parts of Mexico.

These paintings vividly express in visual form concepts of shamanic out-of-body experiences such as bird-like flight and animal transformation by Archaic hunter-gatherer residents along the river 3000-4000 years ago.

Much later, between around A.D. 1050 and 1400, Jornada Mogollon farmers further up river left a detailed record of their beliefs and symbol systems in the landscape, from the El Paso region to central New Mexico. At Hueco Tanks masks and rain gods painted in rock recesses and grottos invoked the power of rain-making forces. At Three Rivers, on a high ridge in the Tularosa Bolson, pecked images of masks, rain gods, animals with symbolic import, cloud iconography, and a variety of geometric designs carried multivocal metaphorical meanings.

In the northern Rio Grande valley Pueblo people also welded the imagery of their beliefs onto landforms, thus confirming their relationship to place and invoking the powers of the cosmos to act on their behalf.

Historically the Athabaskan-speaking Apaches, late-comers on the southwestern scene, also made rock art in the Rio Grande valley in southern New Mexico and West Texas, usually at places where older figures already existed. Finally, evidence of the mission history of the Rio Grande valley can be found painted and carved on rocks here and there throughout the length of the river. Crosses have been added to native symbols, and priests and churches have also been pictured in the contexts of native subjects.

Pecos River style paintings, Texas. These complex rock paintings were made by hunter-gatherer populations who lived in the lower Pecos River region almost 4000 years ago. The paintings themselves have been dated by radio-carbon methods to around 1800 B. C. Archaeologists have identified the elongated anthropomorphs such as the large white figure that is the focus of this painting as shamans, religious practitioners who through a trance state traveled to supernatural realms. Above the head of this figure is a grotesque red serpentine monster that may represent a giant centipede.

Pools and red monochrome figures in Painted Canyon on the Rio Grande

A Pecos River style red shaman with animal profile seems to rise toward a ceiling in Panther Cave, Lower Pecos River region. He carries hunting and ritual paraphernalia including darts, an atlatl, and fending sticks. Other objects defy identification.

The Red Monochrome style from the Lower Pecos River region is characterized by static naturalistic figures painted in a single color. These paintings, superimposed on earlier Pecos River style art work, are dated to after ca. A.D. 600 by the presence of the bow.

Abstracts in red, white, yellow, orange, and black, Painted Grotto, Carlsbad Caverns National Park, New Mexico. These paintings in the Chihuahuan Polychrome Abstract style are also believed to have been made by Archaic hunter-gatherers. Their age has not been determined. Long rows of inverted triangles, strings of dots and linked circles visually tie this painted wall together like an elaborate tapestry. Studies have shown that elements of this nature may picture images seen during trance states. If so these paintings may indicate that this cave was a vision quest retreat.

Detail of the painting of the white shaman, Lower Pecos River Region, Texas. A bird, symbol of spiritual ascent, is attached to the shaman's left arm. He is flanked by flying figures, some with streaming hair. The curved elements to his upper right appear to represent fending sticks.

Petroglyphs and prehistoric impressions, Chimney Rocks, Big Bend National Park. The vulva petroglyph is a common fertility symbol.

Petroglyphs on exposed sandstone face with view to Chisos Mountains, Big Bend National Park, Texas.

Slightly smaller than life-size, a Jornada style mask painted in a water-stained alcove, Hueco Tanks State Park, Texas. Masks such as this one are similar to early Pueblo kachina masks further north. This Jornada Mogollon painting is typical in its broad flat-topped shape and in the use of negative decorative space.

Early historic Apache painting of a shield in white, Hueco Tanks State Park. The figure is about two-thirds of a meter in diameter. Hueco Tanks, with its many water catchment basins, or tinajas, was an important destination and refuge for native people through the ages.

A pair of Jornada style masks from Hueco
Tanks State Park with negatively indicated
facial features. The mouth of the one on
the right incorporates fish iconography and
symbolism. The stocking or pointed caps
suggest that these figures may represent Hero
or War Twins, mythological protagonists that
figure prominently in Southwest mythologies.

Snake, mountain lion, and mask, Rio Grande style, Petroglyph National Monument. In the eighteenth or nineteenth centuries a cross was pecked between the cat and the snake, probably by Spanish shepherds, to nullify the presumed adverse powers of the Pueblo figures.

Over a meter tall, this figure on a basalt boulder in Petroglyph National Monument, near Albuquerque, New Mexico, combines the attributes of a bear and a masked man. The depiction of a bear paw, a powerful fetish used in curing ceremonies, fills the torso. This bear/man figure in outline is an example of the Rio Grande style, a rock art style represented by thousands of carvings and rock paintings in sites up and down the Rio Grande Valley and neighboring regions, and it dates from circa A. D. 1300 to 1680. The Rio Grande style is known for its highly symbolic use of animals, and it is linked historically to the Jornada rock art style that appears slightly earlier in the southern part of the state.

143

Kachina masks are a major feature of Pueblo rock art in the Rio Grande Valley after A. D. 1300. Kachinas are spirit beings with connections to the clouds and ancestors, and they intercede between the Pueblo people and the gods in requests for rain. Kachina masks and an eagle or Knifewing (a sky god based on the eagle), and a shield-bearer cover the sides of this basalt rock. The center mask is pecked across the angle of the rock. To the right a parrot or macaw becomes a headdress of the mask with facial stripes and toothed mouth. Rio Grande Style, Petroglyph National Monument, New Mexico.

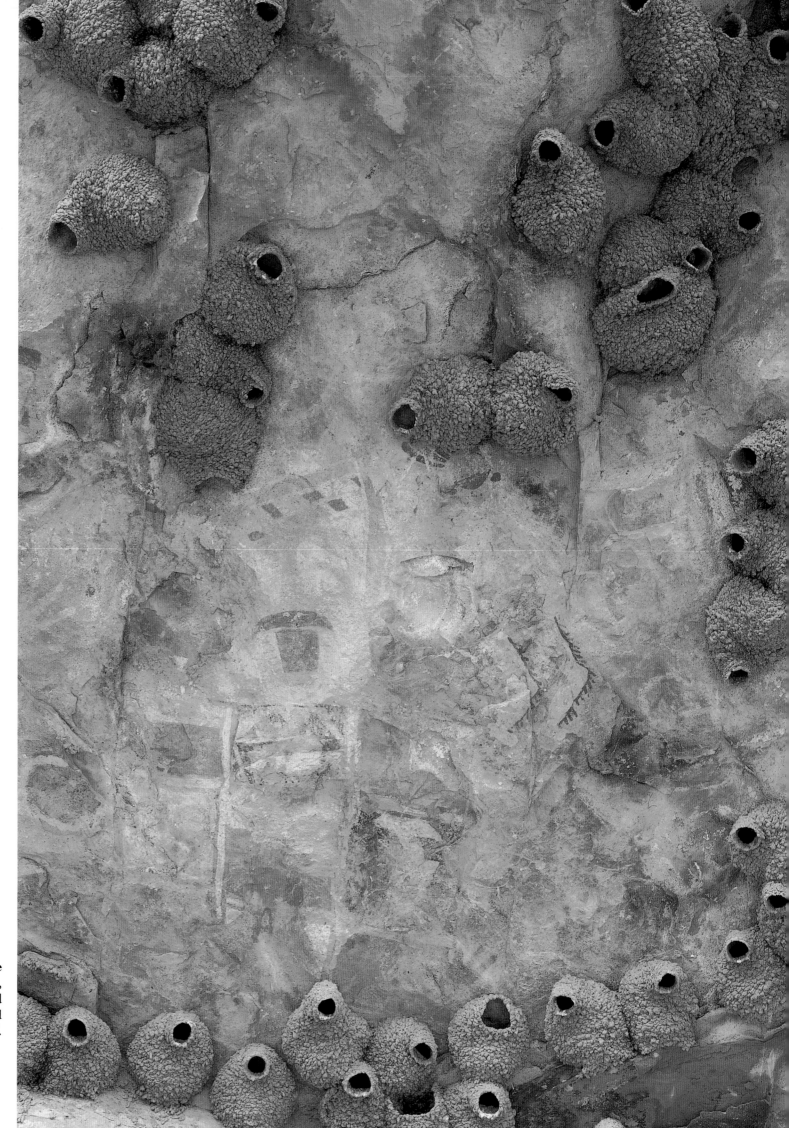

Swallows' nests and Rio Grande style Pueblo paintings, A. D., 1325–1672, Abo, New Mexico. Among the painted elements are a stenciled handprint and masks above a large geometric motif.

Late Pueblo design of unknown significance. A bird, probably an eagle, and a fish appear as smaller figures on this boulder face. Rio Grande style, Petroglyph National Monument.

Abstract masks under a small rock overhang, Abo, New Mexico. Rio Grande style. Painted in thin washes of mineral pigments, these masks have erect feather headdresses and facial designs that incorporate rainbow and cloud elements. The figures approximate life-size.

A pair of feathered, horned
serpents over two meters tall
dominate this rimrock near Abo.
Horned serpents are powerful
Pueblo deities that control
underground water. In the rock
art of the Rio Grande they have
celestial associations as well. In this
panel smaller nearby figures include
a frog, human, and a mask on the
corner of the rock. A second mask
on the upper left-hand corner of
the same rock was stolen by
vandals after 1971.

Petroglyphs of a bear paw,
hand print, two masks
covered with gray lichen,
Abo, New Mexico.

Rio Grande style petroglyphs near Abo, New Mexico. This highly symbolic panel filled with dynamic figures includes a shield-bearing eagle warrior, rattlesnake bear paw print, a mountain lion paw, arrows, a possible arrow-swallower, and other war related symbolism. There are kachina masks as well.

Various Rio Grande style Pueblo ceremonial figures, including kachinas and a stepped line representing clouds. The triangle motif with female fertility implications combines mask and vulva features. The Christian cross is a later addition. Galisteo Basin, New Mexico.

Pueblo shield, a kachina mask, and a ceremonial figure with a flute or arrow, Rio Grande Style, A. D. 1325-1680, Galisteo Basin, New Mexico.

Southern Tewa Pueblo shield-bearers over a meter tall command a section of a high ridge in the Galisteo Basin south of Santa Fe. The figures carry axes, and bear paws and sun symbols decorate their shields. Nearby can be seen a four-pointed star with an eagle feather crest and a warrior with a tall feathered headdress who carries a spear.

Close-up of a carefully pecked shield
on basalt with a border of sun rays.
The interior designs include star faces,
a war-related motif. Rio Grande style,
Galisteo Basin, New Mexico.

Various Rio Grande Anasazi petroglyphs on a basalt escarpment near Santa Fe, New Mexico. A procession of five phallic humpbacked fluteplayers proceed toward a crack in the rock. Across this gap in this miniature vertical "landscape," another phallic humpback holding a staff appears to await the group.

A phallic humpbacked figure blows his flute toward pecked, stepped, cloud motifs. Additional cloud patterns are formed by the negative space between the positive cloud design. Rio Grande style, Santa Fe, New Mexico.

Along the Columbia River at Gingko State Park, Washington, black volcanic rocks bear the pecked images of a pair of human figures with feathered or "sunburst" headdresses consisting of a rayed arc. The hand-held object may be either a small human figure or a stripped conifer branch. The "sunburst," subject to various interpretations, is ubiquitous on the Columbia Plateau, while the "brothers" or "twins" are a common theme within the limited region of the middle Columbia River, and were probably an element of local mythology.

COLUMBIA RIVER

THE Columbia Plateau, encompassing what are today parts of Washington, Oregon, and Idaho, is bordered on the west by the Cascades, the north and east by the Rocky Mountains, and on the south by the Great Basin. The plateau itself was created by horizontal sheets of lava or basalt that form a flat or rolling landscape typically covered by sagebrush, greasewood, and grasses. Willows and cottonwoods border the rivers. This semi-arid open region is cut through by the Columbia River en route from its origins in British Columbia to the Pacific.

From time immemorial until the introduction of the horse in the first half of the 1700s, this landscape was the home of various tribes participating in a fishing-gathering-hunting way of life. Summer camps were often temporary, while residence in the winter was in permanent villages. Ethnographically tribal and linguistic boundaries are complex. The central Columbia from where petroglyphs of the Plateau style are found was occupied by Interior Salish speakers, as well as by Sahaptian-speaking Yakimas. The Cascades formed a barrier between these people and coastal groups. In the Dalles-Long Narrows region where the Columbia leaves the Plateau and cuts through the Cascade Range, Wishram speakers (Upper Chinook) preserve traditional stories about the rock art in the Long Narrows style. Images in this rock art style are analogous to figures carved on stone bowls and other stone implements as well as on antler and bone during the seventeenth and eighteenth centuries. Much of the rock art along the Columbia is thought to be of relatively recent origin.

Paintings in red, white, and yellow-orange on dark gray rock, featuring a variety of rayed concentric elements typical of the Plateau, Columbia River, Washington.

"She Who Watches Over," also known by the Wishram name Tsagaglalal, a legendary figure lightly pecked on basalt in the Long Narrows style, Horsethief State Park, Washington. The face measures 83 x 92 centimeters. An 18th century date is suggested.

Hunter with bow and deer, snake, and hourglass-shaped object pecked on volcanic rock, Plateau style, Columbia River Valley, Gingko State Park, central Washington.

Petroglyphs carved on and near this distinctive granite boulder are thought to have been made in tribute to a power place, signaled by this rock form and its accompanying basin. Pittsbury Landing, Hells Canyon, Snake River, Idaho.

Running bighorn sheep in the Plateau Style, along the Columbia River at Gingko State Park, Washington.

CHUMASH & ANZA BORREGO

THESE distinct regions of southern California have been home to different cultures in the recent and prehistoric past. The Chumash Indians occupied a large region centered on what today is Santa Barbara. Their territory included off-shore islands, long stretches of coast, and the adjacent inland ranges in between which are semi-arid interior valleys. Ecological zones range from high coniferous forests to lowlands that support drought resistant shrubs to the marine environment of the coastal area. Altogether these varied landscapes encompass rich and diverse environments that provided a lucrative living for the Chumash people.

The Chumash were broad-spectrum hunter-gatherers, foragers who depended a great deal upon the wealth of marine fauna as well as a variety of seeds, nuts (acorns and pinyon), berries, and seasonal greens. Among these the acorn was of supreme importance. As a result of the abundance of food resources, the population was relatively dense, especially in the channel area, and villages were large.

The Chumash and their ancestors left a spectacular legacy of rock paintings, made by members of a powerful religious cult known as the 'antap. The 'antap was an elitist group whose members, among other things, acquired ritual knowledge and control and manipulation of

supernatural powers for the purpose of maintaining their society. Their paintings represent Chumash world views and ideological concerns and had several functions. They communicated information about the sacred realm to others, called upon the supernaturals to maintain cosmic equilibrium, and expressed individual experiences of the supernatural gained during vision quests for the acquisition of power.

The Anza Borrego Desert is located south of the Chumash region east and northeast of San Diego in the arid and semi-arid granitic peninsular ranges and desert basins, bordered on the east by the Salton Sea. Ethnographically this region was home to Yuman speakers, the Kumeyaay, whose ancestry goes back into late prehistoric times.

The Kumeyaay consisted of small patrilineal bands of hunter-gatherers who migrated on a seasonal basis from the valley bottoms to the higher elevations of the mountains according to the availability of wild foods. Acorns, and in dryer areas mesquite pods and beans, were major staples, along with pinyon nuts, seeds, and small game. Ethnographically, winter solstice observations, puberty rites, mourning rituals to placate the souls of the dead, and the toloache, or datura, cult figured prominently in their ceremonial life, and it is likely that rock art was made in these contexts.

These colorful rock paintings from the dry coastal and nearby inland ranges of southern California were made in the last few centuries by Chumash Indians who lived in villages and made a substantial living by fishing, hunting, and gathering wild plant foods. Life forms represented in these paintings are thought to be those visualized in trance and associated with super-natural power. These relationships are seconded in Chumash stories and myths.

Black anthropomorphic and red and white bird forms on this surface have suffered from erosion. Los Padres National Forest, California.

Winged shaman figure
in Chumash ceremonial
cave paintings, Burro
Flats, California.

A Chumash lizard with projections
from the mouth or top of the head is
carved and painted in white on a smoke-
blackened background, San Rafael
Wilderness, California.

Paintings in San Emigdio Canyon, believed to be historic in origin, represent some of the most elaborate in the region. Erosion has taken its toll of figures that must at one time have covered the sandstone surfaces of the shelter. Among the motifs represented are life-forms and large sun-like disks with intricate geometric patterns inside. Multiple outlines in contrasting colors around these and other figures contribute to the visual complexity of this art. The circles and other ambiguous symbols are believed to have their origin in shamanic visions induced by the use of datura.

A small Chumash panel painted
in red on yellow sandstone above a
spring near Santa Barbara, California.
Sinuous aquatic life forms, dots, and
large circular motifs can be singled
out in this group.

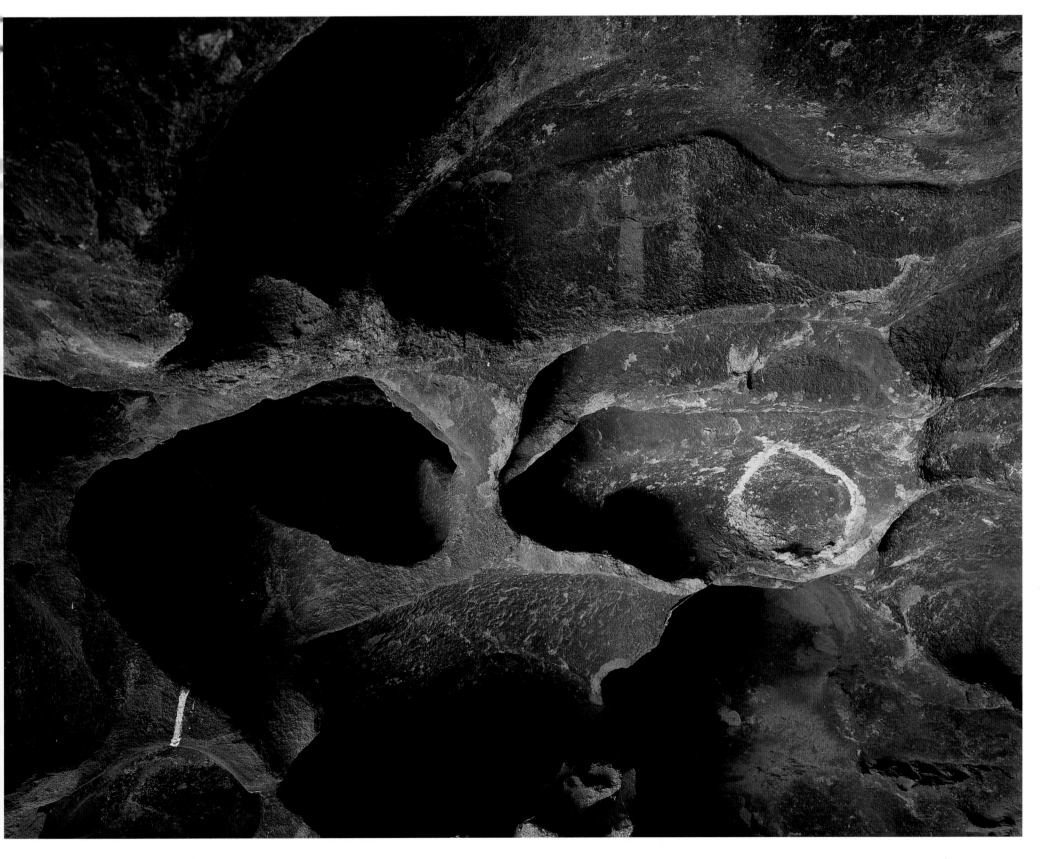

Painted life forms in red on smoke-blackened surfaces in sandstone grotto, Los Padres National Forest, California.

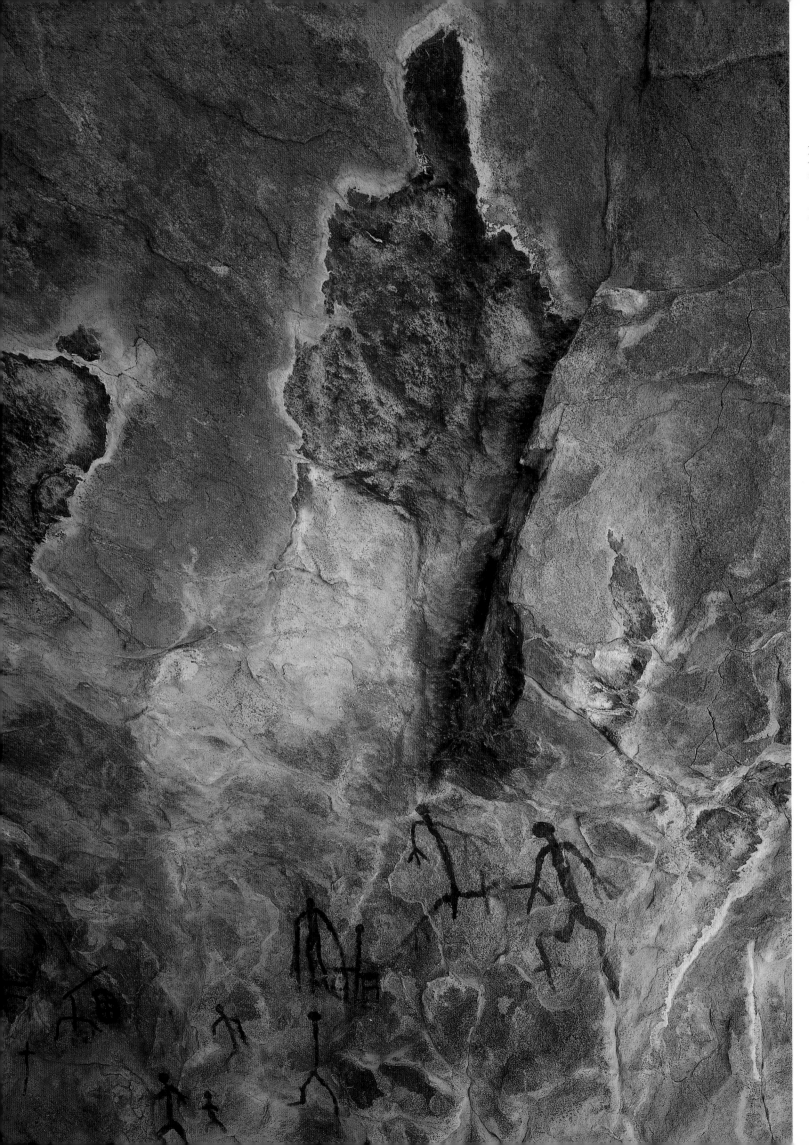

Animated stick figures with round heads on an exfoliating granite surface, Anza Borrego Desert State Park, California. These are attributable to the Kumeyaay, Yuman-speaking hunter-gatherers of the southern California desert.

Chumash Cave Painting, which has suffered vandalism. Painted Cave near Santa Barbara, California.

Chumash life forms express both the bizarre and the familiar. Superimposed paintings in black and red indicate a repeated ritual use of this rock shelter in the Simi Hills, California.

Yellow human figures with splayed fingers and toes are painted on a granite ceiling in Anza Borrego Desert State Park, California. The paintings here are said to have been made by California Yuman, or Kumeyaay, shamans as they prepared for dances.

Chumash ceremonial cave paintings, Burro Flats, California.

The work of Kumeyaay shamans, these abstract motifs in bright red and black are painted near the lip of a granite overhang in Anza Borrego Desert State Park, California. Ethnographic references indicate that these shelters functioned as ritual retreats.

BAJA CALIFORNIA

THE LONG thin peninsula of Baja California, bordered on the west by the Pacific and on the east by the Sea of Cortez, evokes images of sun, desert, and the sea. A broken spine of rough mountains runs the peninsula's length and its climate is variable, but desert vegetation prevails throughout the long central region. The peninsula is well-known for its exotic vegetation such as the cirios, popularly called "boojum trees," various forms of torotes and elephant trees, columnar cacti including the giant cardon and pitahayas, barrel cactus, and various mimosas, agaves, and many others.

For thousands of years hunter-gatherers of Baja made camps around hidden water holes, and exploited the bays and inlets for shell fish, sea mammals and birds, and the mountains for a variety of seeds, roots, and cactus fruits in season. Life was constant, unchanging, and in the dry spring months, often difficult.

The great Central Desert, also known as the Vizcaíno Desert, was sparsely occupied by bands of Indians who spoke a proto-Yuman lan-

guage. At the time of Spanish contact these people were known as the Cochimí. Their archaeological ancestors back a thousand years or more produced an artifact complex referred to by archaeologists as the Comondú culture. Their material goods were simple and consisted of little more than what they could carry, and grinding stones for processing wild seeds were left in place at each campsite.

In the mountain oases in the central part of the peninsula, however, mobile foraging bands developed an elaborate painting style, known today as the Great Murals. In the central sierras, these murals, on the rough rhyolitic surfaces of rock overhangs and shallow caves portray in red and black life-sized men, women, bighorn sheep, deer, and antelope, and birds and sea animals. Thought to have been made in the context of shamanic rituals, these paintings may show shamans themselves in a state of trance with their animal alter-egos, spirit helpers, and guides.

Great Mural Style painting, Cueva Flechas, Sierra San Francisco, Baja California. Here, deer and other animals are represented with shamanic figures, greater than life size. Arrows in this context are thought to symbolize shamanic death, a prelude to trance and travel to supernatural realms.

Polychrome mural paintings on overhang, Cueva Pintada, Sierra San Francisco, Baja California, Mexico.

Palm-lined oases of the Baja sierra once provided water and refuge for Baja's indigenous hunter-gatherers. Permanent water near Cueva Pintada, in the background of this photo, would have allowed groups to congregate and camp in this locality for ceremonies and cave painting.

Large paintings in red and black characterize the Great Murals in the central sierra of Baja California. The Great Mural paintings are thought to be associated with the shamanic traditions of the Comondu archaeological complex, dating between A. D. 300 - 1530. In Cueva Serpiente, Sierra de San Francisco, a long, sinuous serpent is pictured with the head of a deer. Once clearly delineated, the head region is now obscured through the effects of erosion, but ears and antlers are still visible (far right, upper center). Conflated figures such as this are rare in this rock art. The snake is bordered by small bi-colored human figures. In Mexico anthropomorphic figures in rock art are commonly referred to as "monos." Black monos outlined in red are very unusual in the Great Mural style, but the red figure with a roundish body is a distinctive personage who occasionally occurs elsewhere.

Shelter ceilings and walls
provided sweeping surfaces
for the Baja muralists' art.

The bifurcated tail of the serpent at Cueva Serpiente appears at the top of this photo. Small "monos" flank both sides of the length of the snake.

Life-size "monos" in Cueva Pintada
stand with upraised arms, possibly
a trance posture. Male figures are
vertically divided into red and black,
a pattern that may represent body
paint. Females, indicated by the
presence of breasts below their arms,
are each painted in a single color.
Deer rushing as a herd from left
to right contrast with the static
human forms.

**Great Mural Style painting
detail, Cueva Pintada.**

A ceiling in Cueva
Pintada is filled with
superimposed images
of animals and "monos."
The figures seem to
float without reference
to a baseline. Deer,
"monos," and turtle
caparaces delineated
in white are visible.

Granite cave paintings,
Catavina boulder field,
Baja California, Mexico.

Deer and other animals
superimpose life-size
"monos" on the ceiling
of the rock shelter at El
Batequi in the Sierra de
San Francisco. Below, the
once painted vertical wall
is now almost bare. The
pitted surface visible here
is the result of prehistoric

Superimposition of
deer and "monos" at
El Batequi, Sierra
San Francisco, Baja
California

Three Pueblo masks near
the Rio Grande, northern
New Mexico,
A.D. 1325–1680.